THE
Catholic
Digest
BOOK OF
COURAGE

THE

Catholic Digest

BOOK OF

COURAGE

EDITED BY Rawley Myers

MACMILLAN PUBLISHING COMPANY

NEW YORK

COLLIER MACMILLAN PUBLISHERS

LONDON

Macmillan Publishing Company
866 Third Avenue, New York, NY 10022
Collier Macmillan Canada, Inc.

Library of Congress Cataloging-in-Publication Data
The Catholic digest book of courage / edited by Rawley Myers.
p. cm.
ISBN 0-02-588201-5
1. Courage—Religious aspects—Christianity. I. Myers, Rawley.
II. Catholic digest.
BV4647.C75C38 1988
241'.4—dc19   88-19022
CIP

Macmillan books are available at special discounts for bulk purchases
for sales promotions, premiums, fund-raising, or educational use.
For details, contact:

Special Sales Director
Macmillan Publishing Company
866 Third Avenue
New York, NY 10022

10 9 8 7 6 5 4 3 2 1

Designed by Jack Meserole

Printed in the United States of America

To
HENRY LEXAU,
longtime and outstanding editor
of the
Catholic Digest,
with admiration

Contents

II COURAGE OF LOVED ONES: COMMEMORATING THOSE WHO HAVE BEEN EXAMPLES

III COURAGE TO LOVE WITH GOD'S LOVE: REACHING OUT TO THOSE IN NEED

VI COURAGE IN PARENTHOOD: TRUSTING GOD WITH YOUR CHILDREN

VII COURAGE OF THE HANDICAPPED AND THEIR LOVED ONES

IX   COURAGE IN FACING DEATH

Preface

What do we admire most of all? It is courage. This is a book about courage, quiet courage by common people who could well be your neighbors, someone living next door to you. It is the kind of courage and love, beautiful to behold, that many families have. So often their goodness goes unnoticed because our general press is interested in sensationalism. Their courage is not sensational, but it is what holds society together.

History books and newspapers are full of generals and politicians, but the truly great individuals are the people who love, who make this a better world.

Unselfish people like these in this book, and we find them on almost every block, are the mainstay of our communities and nation. We could not go on without them. They don't do things on a grand scale, but they know instinctively that "it is better to light one candle than to curse the darkness."

These people are called ordinary, but they are really extraordinary. They do not get the headlines; they are too busy helping others. They are big-hearted, good-in-soul, wholesome, cheerful; they are "the salt of the earth." Thank God for them.

May the truly heroic lives that we present here inspire many more.

RAWLEY MYERS

I

COURAGE
IN THE FACE OF
CALAMITY

On the Cliff's Edge

My mother had no way of knowing what our tank crew would go through that night, but she had seen it in a dream, darkly

By JAMES G. WOLFGRAM

It was a strange letter my mother had written to me. I wondered if the inspirational message at the end of it was some kind of code to indicate my hospitalized father had taken a turn for the worse. It bothered me especially because in a few hours I'd be back at my unit, the 64th Tank Battalion, trying to turn back the Chinese. It was Korea, 1953.

I wanted to answer her to reassure her that the Panmunjom truce talks would surely result in a cease-fire soon; to tell her that my father would come through his abdominal surgery because of our prayers. But my letter would have to wait. The call was going out to the men to get on the trucks bound for the front lines.

I boarded and read the letter again by flashlight, particularly that ominous underlined epilogue, so totally unlike her usual uplifting Irish sayings. It was the familiar "Lead, Kindly Light" by John Henry Cardinal Newman:

> Lead, Kindly Light, amid the encircling gloom;
> Lead Thou me on;
> The night is dark, and I am far from home,
> Lead Thou me on.
> Keep Thou my feet; I do not ask to see
> The distant scene; one step enough for me.

Why would she write that? I knew she didn't want me to worry about Dad while I was in combat, but why was she so vague? What was she really trying to say?

An hour later the truck screeched to a stop and I clambered out with

3

a buddy to the tune of a high-pitched yell: "Sixty-Fourth, C Company, get out!" The truck lurched on with its cargo of sweating, coughing infantrymen heading for the flashes on the northern horizon. Although it was past 2:00 A.M., the temperature was hovering in the 90's and the dry weather had turned the roads into ribbons of swirling dust. Even the moon had deserted this night of July 12, 1953, as if to leave it to the men below, bent on killing one another.

As our eyes became accustomed to the darkness, we made out the silhouettes of tanks dispersed in the valley below. We groped along toward them, arms interlocked, aware that a blackout had been called. My mother's words struck me again. I wished there had been a light to lead us on then.

I had been the bow gunner (assistant driver) on tank number 21. But when I reached the crew members silently greasing the treads of the big machine, I was told to report to tank number 33. Its driver had been wounded the day before. I reached the tank just as a voice rang out: "We're moving up," and twenty-five engines answered in unison.

I put on my helmet and crawled into the driver's hatch, giving the OK sign to the Korean bow gunner who had started the engine for me. Then my tank commander's voice, that of Sergeant Adolph Fischer, came over the radio: "Good to have you back, Jim. Just follow tank number 32 at a fifty-yard interval. We're going over the mountains to help the 15th Infantry Regiment. They're catching it bad. Keep your hatch open, but maintain radio silence except in an emergency. Just follow the lights of 32."

Follow the lights? This *was* ironic, I thought. My flesh was creeping.

The convoy moved very slowly up the hill to the point at which the truck had stopped, then veered right toward the front and the foothills of the dominant mountain of central Korea, dubbed "Papa-san" because of its height. All the tank drivers knew that this particular road was dangerous even in daytime. There were steep, unguarded precipices, and curves barely maneuverable by a jeep, let alone a forty-six-ton tank.

Lead, kindly light, I thought as I followed the two little red beacons on the back of number 32 up around one curve, then another. The grade was becoming steeper and I slammed the steering stick into low gear and closed to within forty yards of the tank ahead of me. I was losing its lights because its treads and the wind were kicking up a massive dust cloud. There they were again. Thank God.

I glanced at Kim, our bow gunner in the hatch to my right. He had removed his goggles and his dust-caked face looked like a cadaver's. He wiped his eyes, shook his head, and swooped his index finger downward. Yes, Kim, I thought. I know we're on the edge of a mountain but I don't have time to look.

Suddenly, the tail lights of 32 were lost again. The dust was blinding and the wind increasing. If I were to stop, the tank behind me would no doubt smash into ours. I slowed but the wind didn't.

"Keep thou my feet; I do not ask to see . . . One step enough for me . . ."

The words in my brain seemed to herald a terrible chill. I braked the tank, expecting at any moment to feel the crash from behind. What I felt instead was worse. There was a gentle teetering sensation.

I looked down to my right. The lights of the convoy had stopped and flashlights were pointed in my direction. "Dolph," I whispered over the radio. "This is an emergency. I had to stop, but I think we're hanging over the edge of a cliff."

"I know, don't panic," he whispered back. "Send Kim back through the turret. The convoy's stopped behind us. We can get out through the turret hatches, but you may have to climb out and around. Do it easy, Jim; easy, or you'll go over with it."

The engine was still running. I had put the stick into the neutral position without even realizing it. I started to rise but my legs had turned into unfeeling clumps. I slowly sat back down and flicked on the radio switch.

"Dolph, you still there?"

"I'm here."

"I'm going to try reverse gear. Maybe the treads will hold and we can get out."

"The others have left the tank," he said. "I don't think we can try a tow because the tow tank might go over, too. I'm with you. Try it."

My ears were ringing and the horizon seemed to be moving ever so slowly. Far below a bonfire burned. "The distant scene," my mind quoted Newman and my mother again. I hurriedly made an Act of Contrition and eased the driving stick into reverse.

The tank's front dipped downward and my mind's eye saw the middle of the treads grinding the earth. For an eternity, the poets might say, but it was no more than ten seconds, according to the tankers standing on the road behind me as the hulk broke free from the edge and lunged backward. I braked to a stop and Fischer's voice came through again.

"You OK?"

"I guess."

"Let's move out."

I cleaned my goggles and watched Kim crawl back into his hatch. He couldn't speak much English but the full cheeks slowly expelling air were part of a universal language. The message was, "Close call." I gave him one of the same . . . then vomited.

There is a postscript to the story. Although neither I nor my mother again mentioned the quotation in our correspondence, it was my first question when I returned from Korea in 1954.

"I knew when I wrote it that it should be explained," she replied, "but there was no real explanation. I was sitting in the living room writing the letter to you, worrying about you in the war zone and Dad in the hospital, when I began to doze off—not in a deep sleep, but in one of those states where you see things when you close your eyes.

"I knew I wasn't really sleeping and that I wanted to open my eyes, but I couldn't. They were transfixed on a scene I'll never forget. It was either you or your father—the backs of your heads look so much alike—walking down a road, following a light far in the distance. Then the light disappeared along with the human figure.

"I then hovered above a figure—again, it was either you or Dad —and it was writhing, as if in the throes of death. I saw smoky numerals, the numbers three and three, drifting up from the fire. Probably the only thing that saved me from a heart attack when I awakened was knowing that your tank was number 21 and Dad's room number at the hospital was 54.

"Anyway, I went to the kitchen table to finish the letter to you and noticed some literature that had come in the mail that day; a pamphlet with the words of *Lead, Kindly Light*. They seemed so appropriate that I put them in the letter, because the first part of my dream or whatever it was was so beautiful. Later, your Dad recovered from surgery and you came back safely too, so I guess it was just some kind of subconscious trick my mind was playing."

I never told her about my experience on the mountain, nor that I had become a crew member of Tank 33 for the rest of my Korean duty.

Chaplains Who Gave Their Lives

*More than 300 American clergymen have died in battle.
Their example lives on*

By VERNON PIZER

The blacked-out transport *Dorchester* was pushing steadily eastward through the icy waters off the tip of Greenland. It was February 3, 1943. The long northern night had descended and now most of the 904 aboard were asleep below decks. Suddenly the transport shuddered convulsively as a German torpedo smashed through her starboard side. The sea cascaded in through the gaping wound. The vessel began to heel over. From the bridge came the order to abandon ship.

Aboard the dying vessel, men—many of them injured—searched frantically for life jackets, strained to make their way through the debris and rising water in the shattered companionways. Others, in a state of shock, appeared unable to react to the catastrophe. In all the chaos were four pillars of strength, four Army chaplains: George L. Fox, Methodist; Alexander Goode, Jewish; Clark V. Poling, Reformed; and John P. Washington, Catholic. They strove to calm the panic-stricken, to help the confused search for life jackets, to guide men topside, and to aid them into lifeboats swinging out from the tilting deck.

When no more jackets could be found, each chaplain took off his own and strapped it around a soldier who had none. The lifeboats slowly pulled away from the sinking vessel.

Only 299 men survived. Their last sign of the *Dorchester* as she slid beneath the surface revealed the chaplains standing on the canted deck, hand in hand, each praying in his own fashion to the God of them all.

Never had so many chaplains perished at one time and in one place. Americans everywhere, even as they mourned, were inspired by the self-sacrifice of these men of God. Thus in death, as in life, the chaplains continued a ministry that is older than the nation itself.

Though the U.S. military chaplaincy dates officially from its establishment by the Continental Congress on July 27, 1775, chaplains had by then already completed over a century of service with Colonial militiamen. One—David Jones, a Baptist—began his chaplaincy in 1754 with a Delaware militia unit in the French and Indian War, continued through the Revolution as the second chaplain to be commissioned in the U.S. Army, and then, at age 77, ministered to American troops in the War of 1812.

During the Revolution, ten chaplains became prisoners of war, one drowning in an attempted escape; three were slain as they tended the wounded. In the Civil War, seventy-five chaplains gave their lives, fifty with the North and twenty-five with the South. The First World War claimed eleven chaplains. One, a Jew, was mortally wounded at Verdun as he held a cross to comfort a dying Catholic soldier. More than 200 chaplains gave their lives in the Second World War, another thirteen in Korea, while a score more fell serving their flocks in Vietnam.

All casualty statistics are melancholy, but there is a special sadness that surrounds chaplain casualties. Clergymen in uniform threaten no one. Their mission on the battlefield is to nourish life, not to take it. Consider, for instance, Father Vincent R. Capodanno.

Born in New York City in 1929, he entered a seminary in Illinois and finished his studies in Massachusetts. He was ordained in 1957, and the following year he was assigned as a missionary to Taiwan; later he went to Hong Kong.

When the Vietnam conflict erupted into full-scale involvement of American forces in early 1965, Father Capodanno secured permission from his superiors to volunteer as a U.S. Navy chaplain, and asked for assignment to the Marine Corps. (Navy chaplains serve with the Marine Corps and the Coast Guard as well as with the Navy.) His request was granted.

The months that followed were both brutally hard and infinitely rewarding. Never had the priest felt so needed—comforting the wounded, counseling, encouraging, praying with and for his men.

A fellow chaplain said of him, "He was a hungry man. Hungry to be with his troops. Hungry for more time to seek out the lonely Marine; more time to sit with the scared boy; more time to explain things to the confused platoon leader.''

When Father Capodanno's one-year tour of duty in Vietnam expired, he asked for and was granted a six-month extension.

Early on September 4, 1967, in the fourth month of Father Capodanno's extended tour, his company had moved out to probe ahead for the enemy. By midday no contact had been made. The first platoon was leading the sweep. The company command group, with the second platoon in reserve, was following a short distance behind.

The lead platoon was approaching the crest of a rise in the rolling, wooded upland when snipers began firing on it from concealed positions among the trees. Several men were hit and the rest were pinned down. The company's commanding officer sent the second platoon forward to help.

Reaching the crest, the two platoons advanced cautiously for a few hundred yards, meeting only minor resistance. Suddenly, from the front and the flanks, enemy mortars, machine guns and heavy weapons opened up on them. The Marines dived for whatever cover was handy, hunkering down and returning the fire.

The company was facing not merely a few snipers, but a strong enemy force. Outnumbered and outgunned, the embattled Marines radioed back to the company command post that they were in danger of being overrun. The company commander ordered them to fall back and form a defensive perimeter on the hill while he called up a support force from the rear. As the orders were issued, Chaplain Capodanno broke from the command post and ran toward the two beleaguered platoons.

The first man he reached, midway up the slope, lay stunned by a burst of automatic weapons fire. The chaplain, hugging the ground, dragged him up to the defensive perimeter. Then he began moving about the position, offering words of encouragement and helping the corpsmen tend the wounded. The firefight continued unabated but Father Capodanno was intent only on ministering to his men. As soon as he had done all that he could for one group he ran in a crouch to another.

He had already tended a half-dozen of the wounded when he saw a Marine fifty feet away take a hit. Bending low, Father Capodanno sprinted toward him. He was halfway toward his target when a mortar struck close by. Small fragments of the shell perforated his arm and leg and tore away a portion of his hand, but he did not break stride.

He reached the fallen man in time to say the Our Father with him before he died. As the chaplain was closing the dead Marine's eyes, a medic made his way to Father Capodanno to dress his injuries. The priest waved him away, directing him to attend to the more seriously wounded. Spotting a badly hurt Marine trapped between cross fire, Father Capodanno dashed to the man and maneuvered him into a protective depression, where he bandaged the worst of the dazed soldier's multiple wounds.

Then the chaplain witnessed an arresting, wrenching tableau: Lance Corporal Tanke firing at the enemy with one hand while he held his other clamped over the severed thigh artery of a fallen corpsman. An enemy machine gunner spotted Tanke at the same instant and fired a burst that missed. Tanke took aim at his new threat but his weapon jammed. Now defenseless, Tanke scrambled to cover to unblock his piece. Instantly, Chaplain Capodanno raced out and hurled his body between the enemy gunner and the corpsman, at the same time pressing his hand over the thigh artery to stanch its flow.

Hours later, the relief force that had been summoned found the chaplain's bullet-riddled body. His lifeless hand still retained its protective grasp on the man he had sought to save.

The day after he was killed, a letter Chaplain Capodanno had written two days earlier was delivered to Colonel Sam Davis, regimental commander of the 5th Marines. The letter said in part, "I am due to go home in late November or early December. I humbly request that I stay over Christmas and New Year's with my men."

On January 7, 1969, Lieutenant Vincent R. Capodanno, Chaplain Corps, U.S. Navy, was posthumously awarded the Medal of Honor.

Report from Ladder 17

Harold Hoey was a fireman simply doing what he was supposed to do

By DENNIS SMITH*

It is a rainy night in the South Bronx. October 29, 1973, and the streets seem clean beneath the glare of the street lamps. It is 10 o'clock as the voice-alarm system bellows: "Ladder 17, Engine 60, respond to a fire at 420 Willis Avenue."

The fire rages from the windows on the top floor, shooting into the night in defiance of the rain. A New York City fireman, Harold J. Hoey, Jr., badge number 5095, runs along with the captain of Ladder 17 into the building, carrying an extinguishing can and a six-foot hook.

They reach the top floor, and the fire is burning through an apartment door, reaching out into the hall. The men do not take time to harness themselves into masks, and they cough, a little at first, then wildly. Harry directs the can's water at the fire, but it is futile, and the heat envelops them so that they ooze mucus involuntarily from the nose and mouth.

There is one other door on the floor. "Make a search," the captain says, but Harry has anticipated the order. He is at the door, in the wind of the fire across from him, pushing with his full strength.

The door gives, and Harry falls to his stomach, beginning to crawl the length of the hall through the maelstrom of smoke. He is blind, and he gropes until he comes to what he thinks is a bedroom, fifty feet from the door.

He feels a body on the floor. Choking, gasping, he carries it back to the hall. It is a young girl, fourteen, unconscious and barely alive.

---

*Dennis Smith, a New York City fireman, is the author of *Report from Engine Company 82*.

Harry yells, and hands her to a waiting fireman. He turns quickly, and reenters the hall, and the bedroom. On the bed he finds a large woman. He tries to lift her, but she weighs much more than Harry's 180 pounds. His chin and throat are covered with black phlegm, and his coughing is rasped now, and dry. He pulls the woman to the floor, sinking his hands into the flesh beneath her arms, and pulls, a foot at a time, for forty-five feet. He is near collapse when he reaches the outside hall, and he hands the woman over. She is still breathing and it takes four men to carry her in a chair to the street, and a waiting ambulance.

Harry is in the street, walking aimlessly. Firemen try to assist him, but Harry is dazed. "Leave me alone," he says, walking away, looking for a place to regain his breath. The chief orders him to the hospital, gently, with a prideful voice. The chief will write a report requesting a commendation, a medal perhaps.

It is Medal Day for the firemen, June 4, 1974. Along with twenty-nine other men, Harry will be honored. He will receive the Thomas F. Dougherty Medal, and a $100 savings bond for rescuing the woman and young girl. Since Harry worked the night before, there is no time to chauffeur his family into the city. Instead, they will take the train and meet him. Doris is standing there with the boys, Thomas, David, and Christopher, and Harry's mother and father.

The Medal Day ceremonies were once held on the steps of City Hall, with grace and dignity. Today though, as in the past few years, the words of appreciation will echo through the gymnasium of Pace College. The fire commissioner makes a speech, and the mayor makes a speech. There is only one thing to be said, really, to men who have risked all to preserve human life, and that is that they are extraordinary human beings. It is done, and the roll call of the medal winners begins.

Harry's name is called, and he steps briskly to the front. He understands the feeling of great pride that surges through him. He, Harry Hoey, at thirty-four, is being singled out before his wife, parents, and children, and before the gathered firemen, for an act of courage.

Before he went to the South Bronx he had worked for a lighting company, but it bored him. He took a cut in pay to become a fireman because it would not be just a job. It would be a life, a life style.

To say that Harry Hoey is other-directed is like saying that he is

Catholic, or that his father was born in Ireland. It is a fact. He organizes a Christmas party for sixty children in the pediatric ward of Lincoln Hospital. He cooks firehouse lunches for the senior citizens of the Mott Haven projects. Last April, a delegation of senior citizens came to the firehouse. It was a small gesture, they said, but they had pooled their nickels and quarters and had a plaque made for Harry. Harry had been honored then, too.

The mayor pins the medal to his breast, and whispers congratulations, as his wife and boys stand around him. Flash bulbs pop. Harry salutes the mayor, and returns to the ranks.

After the ceremonies, Harry brings his family together, hoping to have a picture taken with his parents and the mayor of New York. There is a crowd around the official. Harry and his family stand at the perimeter, hoping the crowd will diminish. It doesn't. Finally, after much picture taking, the mayor is ushered from the gymnasium, with Harry and his family still on the perimeter. "He is a busy man," Harry says to his father.

It is just eight days later, June 12, 1974. It is a clear night, cool, and a fire has spread throughout the fourth and fifth floors of a half-vacant building. The fire rises up the interior stairs, skirts through the open bulkhead door on the roof, and disappears into the young summer's breeze.

Harry and another fireman, Frank, are in the bucket of the tower ladder. Harry pulls up on a red, six-way control handle, and the bucket lifts the two men, rising on the end of the boom, above the anxious shouts from the street: "People on the roof, man, people on the roof."

Harry brings the bucket fifteen feet above the roof, and he can see a man and woman huddled together, with their dog at their feet, not far from the fire-filled roof door. He is eighty-three. She is seventy-eight. They are shaking.

Harry lowers the boom onto the overhanging cornice. It is a difficult placement. Harry pulls the red handle back so that there will be room to lower the bucket onto the overhang. But nothing happens. The boom is somehow stuck to the cornice. Quickly, Frank climbs over the bucket railing, hangs, and jumps to the roof. The old people are made secure, comforted.

Harry pushes down on the red handle, and the bucket lowers, but the boom is still held to the cornice edge. Harry needs a better angle if they are to get the old couple into the bucket safely. He pulls back hard on the red handle.

Suddenly, violently, the boom separates from the cornice, taking some of the roof with it. The boom flies back. Harry holds the bucket rail with all of his young strength, until it is straight above the bed of the truck, twenty feet from the cornice.

It hangs there momentarily. Now the boom, and the bucket, fly back toward the roof with the force of a thousand torque-pounds. Harry's hands slide from the rail, and it is all over. Harry is catapulted. He caroms from the fire escape, and lands at the base of Ladder 17, lying across the legs that support the fire truck.

The boom steadies, controlled now from below, and Frank and the old couple and the dog are carried safely to the street.

The next morning the firemen of Ladder 17 start a Harold Hoey Memorial Fund, Post Office Box 389, Bronx, New York, 10451.

That day, Doris Hoey donates Harry's skin to be grafted onto the body of a severely burned fireman lying in critical condition.

The nation's heroes go largely unrewarded, except perhaps for a moment's honor, a small ceremony, a plaque, or a medal. The banquets and the silver cups are kept for the famous. Americans have forgotten how to discern between mere fame and heroism.

Our heroes are created by impulses, by dots, by electronic images, and they are honored by book contracts. But if we have a national hero at all he is a judge, or maybe a fireman, who was simply doing what he was supposed to do.

A Father Leaves His Only Son

So that those who are in danger will take courage

By DENNIS C. BENSON

"I've got a story for you." Jim Symons crossed his legs as he sat across the floor from me, and related what an Eskimo friend had told him.

I was about 16. My father, two other Eskimo men, and I were fishing on the edge of the ice. The piece on which we were standing broke off, and very quickly we were pulled out into the Arctic by the currents. Along with wind and weather, it was a very serious situation.

I remember my father's looking at us and saying, "Don't panic, or we die." He proceeded to get into the one kayak that was tied to the ice. I expected to go along with him because I often rode two in the boat, but my father looked at me and said, "Sam, you stay here." Of course, I didn't argue with my father, but I wondered why he would leave me out there.

My father did make it back to the village. Some people had seen the ice break off and had rung the bell. A group of men had brought down some other kayaks. My father tied up three other boats behind him and found his way back to the ice floe. The water that splashed on him froze solid on his body. The only place it hadn't frozen was on his hands because he was pulling the double-bladed paddle.

When Father got on the ice floe, he looked at me and said, "Sam, you choose which kayak you want." This was the first time in my life that Father had said, "Sam, you choose." Always before, I had known adults to take their choice, but this time my father said, "Sam, you choose.'' So I took the kayak that I was used to and paddled back. The two men and then my father returned.

When we made it back to the village, I asked my father why he had left me out there. ''Why didn't you let me go back with you the first time?'' My father looked at me and said, ''Sam, I looked at the other two men, and I was afraid they would panic and die. I knew that if I left my only son there, they would know that I would be back.''

I then asked Father why he had given me the first choice. My father looked at me and said, ''You were a child. Now you are a man.''

A Cliff, a Sea Gull, and a Prayer

Suddenly a large white bird appeared in the sky. Rachel knew her

By FREDERICK JOHN

When Julia and Rachel were very young, back at the turn of the century, their parents taught them the importance of prayer.

"You are talking to God when you pray," said the mother.

"He is always listening," said the father, "and He will answer you when you are truly in need of help."

That is why, even today, Julia and Rachel, now in their eighties, say the rosary daily in their little white cottage on the rugged coastline of Scituate, Massachusetts.

It was also when Julia and Rachel were very young that one of the sisters tossed a rock at a sea gull searching for food on the beach near the cottage. The rock struck the bird, but it had strength in its wings to soar to safety.

"Why did you throw that rock?" the father asked that night, when he heard what had happened.

"Sea gulls are ugly, cackling things," said the rock thrower. "I didn't want the bird on our beach."

"Sea gulls are creatures of God," the father replied. "They are beautiful. God made them, and you must treat them with kindness."

As a result of the rock-throwing incident, Julia and Rachel started taking table scraps to the cliff close by their cottage, and tossing them down on the beach for the birds. In time, one particular sea gull began coming right up on the lawn outside the cottage, in order to be first.

This bird, for reasons known only to the two sisters, was nicknamed Nancy. Later on, Nancy's boyfriend, who became known as Barney, would appear on the lawn as well.

Before the year was over, Nancy showed up at the cottage with a squab. When the original Nancy died, this squab was given her name. The sisters have continued this practice for almost eighty years.

"Today's Nancy is a direct descendant of the original Nancy of years ago," says Julia Flynn. "At least we think she is."

Last October, a chilly, windy day, Rachel, who is a year older than Julia, walked to the edge of the cliff to toss the daily ration of table scraps on the beach. She was wearing only a sweater over her dress, and biting wind made her wish she had on a heavy coat.

Rachel tossed her scraps, and the wind picked them up and carried them out into the choppy sea, where the gulls glided down and grabbed them. But as Rachel turned to leave, the ground beneath her gave way, and she plunged twenty feet down the embankment. Her fall ended when she became wedged between two boulders.

Rachel tried calling for help, but her voice was not strong and nobody heard her. Her fingers groped for her beads in the sweater pocket. But she had left them at home on the small table beside her favorite stuffed chair.

Her knee was throbbing, and her discomfort was increased by the cold. She wanted to pray, but all she could think to say was: "Dear Lord, Good Lord, help me."

Suddenly a large, gray-and-white sea gull came out of the gloomy sky and perched near her on one of the boulders. Rachel knew the bird.

"Nancy," she said, "go get help." The bird flew off.

"Sea gulls are fascinating birds," Julia Flynn picked up the story. "They're loyal to their mates, good parents, and they're smart. Most people think they are pests and scavengers. But they are beautiful, intelligent birds.

"I'll never forget that day. Nancy made a terrible ruckus on the front lawn. I looked out the window, and there she was flapping and cawing like crazy. One time before I saw her carry on that way. It was when they found a whale stranded down on Peggotty Beach.

"I went outside, and Nancy started moving off. She didn't fly, she walked. As she moved, she looked back at me, and kept cawing to make sure I followed.

"I followed Nancy to the edge of the cliff, and down below, I saw my sister, jammed between those rocks. Only the Good Lord knows how long she was down there. I had been busy at home, and didn't even know she was out of the house.

"I called down to her, and she waved her arms so I would know she was all right. She shouted, too, but the wind carried away most of what she said.

"I don't know if she would have died if Nancy hadn't led me there, but it certainly might have been a long time before I found her."

During all this time, the sea gull stood at the edge of the cliff "cackling orders," as Julia put it.

The younger sister rushed back to the cottage and phoned for the fire department. A few minutes later, a rescue team arrived. Ropes, baskets, and medical gear were lowered down, and Nancy glided down to the boulders to supervise the operation personally.

"That bird," said one firefighter, "is smarter than a lot of people I know."

Rachel, it was later determined, suffered a bruised hip, left foot, and left knee. As she was pulled up the embankment in the basket by the firefighters, the sea gull took off and returned to the front door of the cottage to wait for the sisters to come home.

When Rachel had been brought up, Julia Flynn dropped to her knees. "I thanked the Lord," she said, "for watching over my sister. Then I got up and we went home. The men carried her to the cottage, where there was a doctor waiting to check her over.

"I remember Nancy was there cawing away as we came up. Such a beautiful bird. I rewarded her with a little more than table scraps that day.

"Later on, after everybody was gone, Rachel and I said a special rosary. Prayers are powerful. Our parents taught us that eighty years ago."

When the Tornado Took
Our House

*What it's like to watch a storm destroy everything you
own*

By TERESA BLOOMINGDALE

The triple tornado which destroyed our home hit Omaha, Nebraska, at 4:45 P.M. on Tuesday, May 6, 1975. It had been a beautiful spring morning, but by afternoon our spacious skies had darkened and rain was in the air. Nine of our ten children had obediently come straight home from school when teachers told them to "hurry home now, the sky looks strange." Our eldest son, Lee III, was at work, where he had a part-time job in his dad's office.

At 4:00 P.M. Dan, Peggy, Ann, Tim, and Patrick had persuaded me to let them turn on the usually forbidden-on-a-school-day television to watch "The Mickey Mouse Club," which had just made a long-awaited comeback. Our teenagers, John, Mike, Jim, and Mary, were in their rooms studying for final exams.

I was in the kitchen, making hamburger patties for an early dinner, when the kids called from the TV room:

"Hey, Mom, there's a tornado watch on."

I wasn't too concerned. In Omaha tornado watches are as frequent as spring showers. But for some reason, I felt this one might be different; the sky *was* strange, the gray clouds had a greenish hue, so when our fifteen-year-old Jim asked if he could go to the store, just a couple of blocks away, I suggested he wait awhile "just to see what the weather does."

What the weather did was unbelievable, and horrible. At 4:29 the civil defense sirens began to blare, indicating that the tornado watch had been changed to a tornado warning. A funnel had been sighted. Even then we didn't seek shelter (we would today; on that day we learned a profound respect for that siren), but four minutes later, at 4:33, another bulletin reported that a funnel had touched down in southwest Omaha, causing undetermined damage. It was then that I ordered the children to the basement. The little ones scampered downstairs immediately; the teenagers, however, insisted on standing at the southwest dining-room window, watching the sky grow even blacker as the wind began to whip the trees.

A few seconds later they saw the funnel, a massive cornucopia of dark debris, whirling directly toward our three-story, nineteen-room home. For one awful moment they were paralyzed, and terrified, as they hypnotically watched that funnel snatch up houses and cars, and hundreds of appliances from the huge Sidles warehouse on 74th and Pacific, southwest of our home. Finally Mike and Jim tore themselves from the terrible sight and dashed to the basement, tripping over each other in an effort to reach shelter.

"What's it doing out there?" I asked Mike. I wasn't frightened; I had never been in a tornado before; I had never even been close to one. I thought if we were hit, we might lose a few shingles off the roof or even a couple of windows. "What did you see?"

"One helluva funnel," said Mike, "and it's headed this way."

And indeed it was. When it was still a mile away we could feel the pressure on our skin, as if we were being squashed by some invisible force. The noise was incredible. I had heard that the noise of a tornado is comparable to a loud freight train; this is true only in that it goes *clack-clack-clack*. I have never heard such a terrible sound. It came like a thousand jets at rooftop level, the roar accompanied by banging and battering, twisting and tearing.

The triple funnel first tore through Bergan Mercy Hospital, where nuns and nurses had quickly moved patients to shelter, and where Dr. Joseph McCaslin, treating a heart patient in the emergency ward, courageously continued with emergency cardiac care which saved his patient's life.

The funnel then sliced through Sidles, removed the top floor of the newly built, luxurious 7400 Plaza Building, and then turned east to 72nd Street only to veer north again to terrorize but not injure 9,000 spectators at the Aksar-ben race track. It whirled back and forth across

72nd Street, leveling the mammoth, multi-million-dollar Nebraska Furniture Mart and ripping apart the solid brick Farmer's Union Insurance Building.

Then as if seeking another juicy victim, it spotted our big white house on a 70th Avenue hill, and it struck.

The electricity exploded, leaving our basement shelter in total darkness, and then I did panic. I had forgotten to turn anything off; we had a gas furnace, gas stove, and gas hot-water heater. I waited for another explosion. (It did not come.) As I fought hysteria, I suddenly became aware of the incredible calmness of my children.

Mike, Jim, and Mary had reached for a younger sibling and held tightly to eight-year-old Annie, seven-year-old Tim, and our youngest, Patrick, who was only five. Danny, eleven, and ten-year-old Peggy had always been close siblings, but never so close as they were at that moment, clinging to each other. Our toy poodle, Mimi, shivered at my feet, as terrified as the rest of us. I gave a brief thought to Dolly, our aging Irish Setter, who had been sleeping on the front porch. Where was she now? (She was under the porch, scared but safe; she survived.)

The roar was even louder as the funnel rolled back our huge Spanish-tile roof and sucked our entire third floor into its mouth. Every door was slammed, again and again; every one of our sixty-seven windows was shattered and then sucked into the funnel, leaving a blanket of glass shards across the plowed-up lawn.

Furniture was hurled from room to room, from block to block, and replaced by heavy filing cabinets and computers from a neighboring bank.

We didn't know all this immediately, of course. All we knew was noise, and that terrible pressure inside our heads and outside our bodies.

How long did it last? A few seconds? Minutes? Forever? I honestly don't know. Too long, that I do know. It was over suddenly, shockingly; and the silence was all around us, eerie and weird and as frightening as the noise that had preceded it.

I couldn't bring myself to go upstairs. I made our seventeen-year-old son, John, who had brazened out the storm in his basement bedroom, go first, and we cautiously followed. As he forced open the door leading into the kitchen, he paused a moment, then said softly, "Oh, my God."

The kitchen was a shambles; our huge double-oven stove now stood in the center of the room; cabinet doors were blown off; yet, incredibly, my crystal goblets stood untouched in those same cabinets.

In the dining room our ten-foot refectory table had been crushed under the weight of a giant oak tree, which had sailed through the wall, leaving a gaping hole. Furniture was disarranged as if a devil had moved it by a magic spell, smashing it against the walls, even moving some of it into the next room.

In our living room, every piece of furniture was ruined. A heavy typewriter which had been resting on a card table in the corner was gone; we never did find it. A strange bicycle stood in the center of the room; we had no idea to whom it belonged. A soiled apron, not mine—a neighbor's, I presume—hung from a picture hook where a portrait of the Sacred Heart had formerly graced our home.

I looked out the windows that were no longer there and tried to cry, but I couldn't. For blocks around us homes had been leveled, trees uprooted, shrubs stripped bare. I thought of the family behind us, with seven little children. Were they all dead? Was everybody dead?

Nothing moved. No one appeared. The silence was terrifying. Later we realized the strange quiet was due to the death of nature: there were no leaves left to rustle; no insects to hum; no birds to sing. I have never heard before or since the terrible "sounds of silence" we heard that day.

The silence was suddenly broken by a crash of thunder, followed by a cold, heavy rain bringing with it hail and more wind. With no windows and no roof, the muddy water ruined the few things that might have been saved.

Having finished the destruction, the rain quickly followed the tornado which had preceded it; the skies cleared, and a bright May sun shone on our shattered world.

Slowly, cautiously, as if they were afraid of what they would find, the neighbors began to appear on what remained of their porches and patios. For one moment we simply stared at each other, then they called:

"Are you all right? Is everybody all right?"

"Yes. Are you?" Yes. Miraculously, we were all right. Only three people were killed in the tornado, which had continued north up 72nd Street, demolishing part of Creighton Prep, our Jesuit high school, destroying Lewis and Clark Junior High, a synagogue, the Omaha

Community Playhouse, churches, stores, homes, and office buildings. In all, it devastated a total of 900 square blocks and left 300 persons injured, though none of them were in our block.

Within minutes the streets filled with people, some coming to help, others to gawk and even to loot.

As I made my way across our living room, a young man dashed through the front door, stared at us, and suddenly began to cry. His tears were quickly replaced by an embarrassed grin, as he said:

"I saw your house blow away. I was watching from our house (four blocks away) and I saw your third floor just go. I thought you were dead," said Mike Rouse, a senior at Prep and a classmate of our son John. Almost immediately, from the other direction, Mike's married brother Jim came running toward the house, carrying a desperately needed flashlight, for while dusk had not yet fallen, our basement, where gas and water had to be shut off, was pitch black.

As I headed back through the house toward the basement, a red-bearded giant climbed through a window shouting: "Anybody here injured?"

"No," I answered. "We're all right." This complete stranger then threw his arms around me and hugged me, as if to thank me for not being dead. Then, as quickly as he had come, he departed, through the same window, to continue his search for someone in need of help or a hug.

Others were not so concerned; they had come to sight-see and to scavenge. My shock turned to fury as I watched these idiots carelessly light cigarettes around overturned cars and broken gas mains. Who knew what explosive fumes might be in the air? But God blessed us: there were no explosions, no fires. Just sight-seers and scavengers, crowding the streets to the point where it became impossible for husbands and fathers to reach their destroyed homes.

Husbands and fathers! Panic really hit me as I thought of my husband and son. Where were they? How far had the tornado gone and in what direction? Had it hit my husband's office? Were they safe? Why didn't they come home?

I learned later that my husband was at his office, desperately trying to call home. But the lines were down; he could not get through. He finally contacted a neighbor, half a mile away, and asked her if the tornado had hit our area. She couldn't bring herself to tell him that she had seen our house demolished. She said simply: "You'd better go home."

It took my husband and son almost two hours to travel two miles; it was not so much the debris that blocked the streets, as it was the people. They finally left their car and walked the last quarter mile home.

Meanwhile, I was terrified, not knowing where they were and also fearing my husband's reaction to the dreadful sight. I made all nine children stand in the middle of the street so, when he turned the corner, my husband would see that we were safe.

Finally I saw him, and I watched his face contort in fear as he saw the beautiful home he had provided for us, now a blackened mass of crumbling stucco and broken glass. His steps quickened, and I realized he hadn't seen us; he didn't know where we were, or even *if* we were.

I ran to him, tripping over fallen electrical cords and felled trees, pushing my way through strolling sightseers and stunned neighbors. I threw myself into his arms and finally, at last, I cried.

"We're all right," I sobbed, repeating that beautiful phrase over and over. "All the children are here; we're all right. But our house . . . is gone. Oh, honey, I'm sorry! Our beautiful home is gone!"

He held me tightly and smiled. "Sorry? Honey, it's not your fault!" (A family joke: everything that goes wrong is Mom's fault.) "Come on now," he said, "let's get the kids together and go home."

"Home?" I asked.

"Yes," he said calmly, and forced a laugh. "Home. I'm not too sure where home will be, but I promise you, I'll take you home."

And he did. It's a different house, of course, without a familiar piece of furniture in it. But with the same family, all safe and all together, it's home.

It took weeks before we saw any humor in that tornado, but, it being my tornado, I knew there had to be some. And there was.

The first laughter came when a reporter interviewed me and asked: "What was your first thought, your first reaction, when you came up out of your basement and saw the damage and destruction?"

It was such a typical newspaper-reporter question, we had to laugh. But being from a newspaper family, I appreciated the reason for his question, and tried desperately to remember my reaction and to give him a newsworthy answer.

Before I could come up with a headliner, Timmy broke in and said:

"I remember, Mama. You looked around the living room a minute and then you said: 'Somebody get a broom; we've got to get this mess cleaned up before your father gets home.' " I don't believe that, but the kids swear it's true.

We all laughed again, a few days later, when the insurance inspectors were assessing damage to our house. When they got to the basement, they opened the door of John's bedroom and exclaimed:

"My God! It really went through here. What a mess!"

That was the only room in the house that the tornado hadn't touched.

II

COURAGE OF LOVED ONES: COMMEMORATING THOSE WHO HAVE BEEN EXAMPLES

A Lady Shows Her Mettle

There was starch in that old lace

By BARBARA COX

Her generation shuddered when a woman's name appeared in print on other than socially acceptable occasions (birth, wedding, funeral). So my mother will be jolted to learn that her life to date is laid bare in the three press clippings here on my desk. Worse, they could eventually apply to anyone's mother who has survived the safari from pre-1900 through the twentieth-century jungle.

1913: "The bride was strikingly beautiful. . . ."
1948: "The deceased leaves his widow. . . ."
1978: "Woman, 86, assaulted."

I'd like you to know her better. Mother was and is reserved in manner, befitting the daughter of a Quaker minister. Why, then, did my bluff, outgoing father—a lion in his business and a blatant liar after his fishing trips—remain docilely in her domestic web from the moment he fell in love with her at Sunday Meeting until the last breath of his life?

No doubt her dark red hair (they called it auburn in those days) had something to do with it, to say nothing of the translucent complexion.

There was a full autumn moon the night of the wedding, and the local society editor went slightly mad with the romance of it all. The flourishing finale came when the bride and bridegroom departed for their honeymoon in—brace yourselves—an automobile. What the writer didn't know was that my mother had been told the facts of life by her own mother only a few hours earlier, in the family buggy on the way to town. You'll note, however, that she went through with the ceremony.

Mother is still annoyed when we tell her that she became an immaculate housekeeper, but she did. The rooms shone, her sewing was pure art, her cooking prodigious. But never once did my father return at night without finding her in a freshly laundered white bib-apron over a prim shirtwaist and skirt, serenely preparing dinner.

"Frankly, dear," she told me later, "when I ran out of time I simply put a covered pan of water on the stove to boil. He only *thought* it was dinner."

I still have her handwritten recipes: "Mrs. Lawrence's Luncheon," "Mrs. Wood's Bridge Refreshments"—her closest friends, but not even on recipe cards would she use their first names. Small wonder they went into shock when, in the middle of the raging debate over flappers and short hair, my mother slipped quietly into the nearest barber shop and came home with the first "bob" on the block.

She gave birth to three children and lost another, faced the Depression with her chin high, left parents and life-long friends forever to bring her husband across a continent when his failing health required the climate of southern California. Widow, grandmother, great-grandmother—then two crippling strokes, and the proud fortress seemed to crumble.

She must have looked very small to the man outside her room in the retirement home that night. Small and helpless, an ideal victim. Painfully, she pulled herself up from her armchair and faced him as he ripped the screen its full length and forced his way through the French door, dropping the rope meant to silence her. No need for it. This would be easy.

Easy? Her screams shook the walls. He tried to cover her mouth, but she refused to stop. Helpless? He pushed her down, and still she screamed. ("Frankly, dear, I considered biting him but decided screaming would be more useful.")

He reached frantically into his pocket and brought out his knife.

It was raised and ready when a woman from a neighboring room threw open the hall door. (Senior citizens, they call these people. The title is an accolade.) "Out!" the woman ordered. "Get out!" Only when the knife was turned on her did she retreat, but by then the passageway was packed with the infuriated elderly. The attacker made his only brave move of the evening. He pushed through them to escape.

* * *

Our family is more shaken than my mother. ("Frankly, dear, I can't see the need to move. No place is perfect.") We had surrounded her with love and protection, but it wasn't enough. In the end she saved herself.

Somewhere my father is laughing. He knew the girls of 1913.

My Polish Parents

They wouldn't give in

By REGINA GODZISZ-KOŚCIELSKI

Felek and Teklunia have the same motto as that of another Polish-American, the pianist Artur Rubinstein: *"Nie dam sie!"* Translated loosely it means, "I won't give in!" And they didn't.

Felek and Teklunia were runaways, escapees, liars. Most Poles who came to America in the early 1900's, especially those from Polish Russia and Polish Germany, had to lie, because restrictions on travel were severe. So they lied about their ages, their reasons for crossing a border, their very names.

Felek was nineteen, the age of Russian conscription. He had been detained six months for questioning as a suspected member of a Polish underground organization. He was not a member, and was released, but his friends and family feared for his safety. So he obtained a pass to Austrian Poland on the pretext of visiting an aunt. From there, he left for America.

Teklunia was sixteen, the eldest of six children. Her widowed mother needed help with work on the land and in the house. The solution was a simple, common one: marry Teklunia off to a strong worker, who would live with his mother-in-law and work her land. An aunt in the next village knew of a man who was willing and made the arrangements. Teklunia rebelled. The thought of marrying a stranger was repugnant to her. So one morning she started off, presumably to her daily chore of milking the cow, left the milk cans behind the stable door, and walked out of the village to meet some friends who were leaving for America.

Felek and Teklunia found the passage across the ocean pleasant enough. The food was good, for those who were able to keep it down. They were treated well. Coming from abject poverty, they did not expect luxury on board ship and were not particularly aware of overcrowding or inconveniences.

One landed in New York, the other in Montreal. Both cities had similar procedures for immigrants. There were translators, and people who would put them on the right trains to the right destinations. But Felek did not like the identification tag which all had pinned on their clothes. So he tore his off and threw it away. This caused some difficulties, such as having to take a taxi and being overcharged.

Then began the new life in America: living in boarding-houses, looking for work, working harder than they ever had in Europe, making foolish mistakes, being insulted ("Polander" was the prevalent term of derision then), being misunderstood because of the language barrier, sometimes being laughed at, more often being helped. Eventually, both came to Detroit, where they met and married.

Saving a down-payment on a home in a Polish neighborhood was of prime importance. Then the monthly payment was always the first thing taken from the meager paycheck. They shared the heavy work around the house. When a load of coal was delivered, Teklunia shoveled it into a wheelbarrow and then into the coal bin, saving the twenty-five cents a ton wheeling-in charge. She helped lay sidewalks and put up fences. Many a bitter neighborhood feud had started over boundaries, so their fences were installed very carefully: not an inch was taken from or given to the neighbors.

There had to be a garden with carrots, parsley, onions, beets, and tomatoes to be eaten in season and canned and stored for the winter. There had to be a lawn, neatly trimmed and weeded. There had to be flowers, many different varieties for continuous bloom and for trading with the neighbors. Seeds were gathered and stored for the next spring: one could not afford to buy flower seeds every year. During the spring and summer, to keep the vegetables, flowers, and lawn thriving, there was the daily ritual of watering, even when it rained. Only a downpour warranted skipping a day.

Felek had learned a trade in Poland, tile stove fitting, which was useless in America. So he did factory work. Those were pre-union days, when working conditions were truly difficult. Frequently he complained about his foreman and company policies, but he was proud of his contribution to the auto industry. When he saw a Cadillac on the road, he would say, "There! My work is on that Cadillac. Every fender of every Cadillac is welded by me. I do a good job!"

Felek did all his own work around the house: electrical, plumbing, painting, carpentry. He cut his children's hair, and repaired their shoes. When you cannot afford to hire someone, you learn to do it yourself.

Teklunia, too, was proud of herself as a worker. Before her marriage, when she was hired as a dishwasher in a restaurant, she burned her hands because she made the water too hot, determined that those dishes would be really clean. During the Depression, when the going got rough, she worked in a hotel, washing floors, windows, toilets. Many a fine lady requested that she be her permanent cleaning woman.

This Polish-American couple was never too proud to do any kind of honest work. They were too proud only to ask for help, to "go on welfare." Asking for help from the Welfare Department was the final, most desperate step a family took. Felek and Teklunia worked hard, scrimped, and denied themselves to avoid such a calamity. They succeeded.

America was a good place. They were making progress while their families in Poland were standing still. They felt homesickness for loved ones but no yearning to return to their past living conditions. America was their country now.

To become an American citizen, Felek went to night school to learn English. By that time they had children, and it was their ten-year-old daughter who drilled her father in the possible questions the judge might ask about the Constitution, the three branches of government, who was the first president, who was the present governor. Felek studied, he worried, he passed the test. He received the precious citizenship papers.

Teklunia did not think papers were that important. She was here, she felt American. Then came the Second World War. She had to register as an alien. "I have two sons in the Army and they say I'm not an American?" She registered as an alien one day and applied for citizenship the next day. But she did not pore over any books. Felek worried. "You won't pass. You're not studying about the Constitution!"

"Don't fret. I read the newspapers; I listen to the radio; I know what's going on. And I have two sons in the Army!" She made it.

No national holiday goes by without Felek hanging out the American flag on the front porch. The neighbors have a friendly contest going: who will be the first to display the flag on the morning of a holiday? Shame on the one who forgets to bring it in by dusk!

They both vote, every election, without fail. And, of course, they vote straight Democratic. No newspaper editor, no radio commentator can change that. After all, President Wilson was a Democrat, and he put Poland back on the map with his Thirteenth Point after the First World War. And Franklin Roosevelt saved the home when it was almost lost during the Depression. Roosevelt was for the working man. Democrats are always for the working man. Republicans are for the rich people. So they vote straight Democratic!

The Church was important to them. They believed that no Church ever taught anyone to do bad things, so all churches were good. But since they were born and raised as Catholics, they went to the Catholic Church. They felt that not all priests were good. But there were those priests *z powołania* (with a true vocation), whom they admired and supported.

Nuns, on the other hand, were *all* dedicated, holy women. As teachers they were unsurpassed. Felek and Teklunia, along with their contemporaries, truly believed that Polish parochial schools, taught by these good nuns, gave children a far better education than public schools could. What other proof was needed than that these parochial schools taught their children Polish and catechism as well as English?

Education was important. They appreciated its value because they had had so little. Teklunia never went to school at all. She was taught some reading and writing by her father. Yet now she reads both Polish and English fluently. Felek went to school only two winters, but he reads constantly and writes beautiful letters. He believed education was very important—but not for girls.

For his sons he would have done anything in the world, made any sacrifice, to put them through school. For his daughter—why go to high school? You will finish at eighteen and get married. What good will high school be then? Music lessons, yes (you might attract a better man), but high school for a girl—no!

They did not read stories to their children, but many an evening was spent in reminiscing about the Old Country, personal experiences, history, legends. Felek knew many poems and songs and shared them, and taught them to his children. He knew little rhymes which mentioned boys and girls with the same names as his children. What embarrassment to his daughter when she recited one of these poems in school and learned that the name of the girl in the original poem was not the same as hers.

Holidays were observed in a traditional Polish manner. *Opłatek* at Christmas, *pisanki* at Easter. Herring, beet soup, and the rest for Christmas Eve *Wigilia* supper, white *barszcz, kiełbasa*, eggs, and home-grated horseradish for Easter breakfast.

On Christmas Eve, some Polish-Americans left an empty place at the table for the Christ Child. Not they. Rather, they invited someone to share their meal: a bachelor uncle, a lonely neighbor, a widowed friend. This was proverbial Polish hospitality: *"Gość w domu, Bóg w domu"* (a guest in the home, God in the home) and *"Czym chata bogata, tym rada"* (what the cottage is rich in, that it is happy to share).

American customs were quickly and happily accepted. Santa Claus, Halloween (pennies for the beggars), Thanksgiving turkey, Mother's Day, Father's Day, Decoration Day, Fourth of July.

Their ties to Poland remain. Letters are still exchanged regularly. They help their families with packages and money. They are interested in the political situation. They reminisce often. Their children are grown and they have been financially secure for many years.

A trip to Poland is within their means and has been suggested often, but they refuse. For one, they think they would be overcome with emotion. The sight of those remembered fields and forests, wayside shrines and stork nests, the village church and cemetery, the family cottage with its thatched roof, the people and the sounds of their regional speech would overwhelm them. "We would not come back, we would die there!" Besides, when they left Poland it was without any thought of returning. They were content.

Despite the bad times, when they had to struggle, when they had difficulty making ends meet, through illnesses and worries, America has been good to them. Although they are proud of their Polishness, they are now Polish-Americans with the accent on American.

At the ages of eighty and eighty-three they are still true to their unspoken motto. They will not give in to old age, to aches and pains, to loneliness. They are still active, still independent, still determined to make their own decisions and live their lives in their own way. *"Nie dam sie"* is a good motto. With love, admiration, and deepest respect I, their daughter, accept that motto and recommend it to my children —their grandchildren.

For My Housekeeper, Meriam Lux

What is holiness except the charity and generosity that she lived?

By HENRY FEHREN

Last spring in a lonely, unmowed cemetery, near a windswept village in Minnesota, a holy woman was buried. Her name was Meriam Lux and she had been my housekeeper for twenty-two years.

I say holy woman, for I can testify to twenty-two years of her holiness. She did not know that she was holy, and she would be uncomfortable if she knew that this sort of thing was going to be written about her. But what else is holiness except the charity and generosity that she lived?

When Meriam Frances Lux was born in 1900 (on the feast of St. Francis Xavier, as she always pointed out), her health was so fragile that the doctor who came to the farm to deliver her predicted her imminent death. She survived, but a brother and sister born later both died in childhood. There were no other children in the family.

When Meriam was a sophomore in high school, she had to quit her studies to take care of her mother, who was dying of cancer. She then took care of her father until he died. Suddenly she was left alone.

A sick woman in Colorado Springs needed help; Meriam went out there. The Irish pastor of her home parish needed a housekeeper; she went back there and kept house for him for nine years. On his retirement she became housekeeper for a kind but gruff priest of German extraction. When the bishop volunteered him into the army as a chaplain, Meriam took on the care of a doctor's mother.

About this time I had been pastor of my first parish for seven months and was tired of my own cooking—cornflakes and hot dogs. I tried to fry eggs but they always ended up scrambled.

So Meriam's letter of application was most welcome. Another housekeeper had told her of my plight. When I drove over to pick her up and saw a small figure crumpled up on a sofa I had second thoughts. "Doesn't look too bright," I said to myself smugly.

I asked her only one question, "Can you bake bread?"

"I haven't for some time," she replied meekly, "but I can try."

So I showed her the back seat of the car and carted her off to my parish. Praise God from whom all blessings flow. I soon realized how good He had been to me.

For Meriam Lux was all that a housekeeper should be and then some. She was an excellent cook, though if anyone asked her for the recipe of something she had made, she could give only vague instructions. Her bread was unequaled. I told her that my many visitors came not to see me but to eat her bread.

She served all priests, no matter what their personality, habits, or attitudes, equally well. "I'm working for the Lord," she would say. That she kept house for me for twenty-two years is enough to merit her canonization.

No matter what scandals or changes there were in the Church, her faith remained unwavering. Not once in the years I knew her did I hear her complain about the Church.

Her generosity was legendary. She simply gave away everything. "Money just causes trouble," she said. She never heard of voluntary poverty but she practiced it. There were never more than a few dollars in her old purse.

A housekeeper's salary is below the poverty level, but the Internal Revenue Service investigated her in 1968. They said she listed too much for charity in comparison to her salary. I sent them her canceled checks and showed that she had not even listed all her charities in her income tax report. I could see why a report like hers could send an income tax computer into a tizzy.

What few clothes she had she wore until they were shabby. She was not about to spend $15 on a new frock when someone else needed help. Yet if someone gave her a ride to a meeting of the ladies sewing for the missions, she wanted to pay for the ride. She did not drink or smoke, but on rare occasions, when she was fatigued from a day at the ironing board or in the vegetable garden, she would offer to pay for a cold beer from my supply.

She worked seven days a week year round, and took off only two days twice a year to visit her home village. She would always stop at the rectory there to leave an offering for the care of her family's graves.

She never grumbled when extra guests came in at the last minute for dinner. The food was still hot and on time. She once said jestingly that what I called a rectory was more like a hotel.

She had a beautiful humility. She always sat in the back seat of the car, ate in the kitchen (usually leftovers), never interfered in the parish, and did not get involved in parish gossip. In twenty-two years I never heard her say an unkind word about anyone.

Physically she was not beautiful. She was small, and she became hunchbacked in her later years. Her feet were bad, so she seemed to walk in all directions at once. Her clothes always seemed to hang haphazardly on her shapeless form, and her slip was always showing. She just laughed about these things.

Indeed, she was always cheerful, even during some times of great difficulty. I cannot tell of those times because others involved are still living. But even when she was cheated she did not complain. She always sensed that she was in the hands of the Lord and He would take care of her.

She worked until inoperable cancer forced her into a rest home and then a hospital. I visited her in the hospital before her death. Her mind was clear and we discussed arrangements for her funeral. Since she had no close relatives (indeed, she rarely had any visitors), she asked me to take care of her will. And she asked that when the ground was put back upon her lowered coffin some of it be put on the graves of her parents, for the graves were sinking.

De mortuis nil nisi bonum—of the dead speak nothing but good—is an ancient Latin proverb. It is one easy to fulfill in Meriam's case. She was simply a totally good person. Her way was the "little way" of St. Therese. She followed Christ closely, and I was privileged to have her as housekeeper.

So I write of her, not to give tribute, which she can no longer hear, but to point out to the spiritually fainthearted that a life of humility, love, and faith is possible. Meriam lived and died in peace because she accepted Christ's call to follow Him.

She sensed that the single life was her vocation from God and she was content with that. Much attention is given in sermons and Church publications to family life, but Meriam showed that the single life is equally important and useful in the eyes of God.

"There are different gifts but the same Spirit; there are different ministries but the same Lord," writes St. Paul. "There are different works but the same God who accomplishes all of them in every one. To each person the manifestation of the Spirit· is given for the common good." Meriam accepted the gifts God gave her and used them for good.

One of my favorite passages in the Gospel is especially applicable to Meriam. It is the one where Christ says, "It will go well with those servants whom the Master finds wide awake on his return. I tell you, He will put on an apron, seat them at table, and proceed to wait on them" (Luke 12:37). It is good to know that this woman who served the Lord faithfully for a lifetime is now being waited upon by Him.

III

COURAGE TO LOVE WITH GOD'S LOVE: REACHING OUT TO THOSE IN NEED

A Family That Passed Our Way

Good deeds have a way of multiplying

By DIANNA DANIELS BOOHER

Evicted, are you sure? Well, I can't believe anyone would do that. That old landlady has more money than she knows what to do with, and she's ordering a mother and four kids out in the street?" I listened to the pastor as he told me the details of Margaret's plight. As I hung up the phone, I was indignant.

Then I began to think along more practical lines. Margaret and her four children, ages two, four, five, and seven, would be without a home in two days. What could I do? I could always call and say I was sorry. And I truly was.

Margaret didn't have a resident husband. Mark was an alcoholic. Their marriage had been a nightmare for the last few years. Mark would come home, hold a job for a month or two, and then he would leave again. Margaret seldom knew where he was.

The children looked to their mother as the stabilizing force in their lives, and she had always managed to shield them. She couldn't shield them from this, though.

Margaret and I were friends, but when I considered our relationship, I began to wonder how loosely I was using that word. I knew Margaret's parents had died some years before, but surely she had someone, some family, some friend closer than me to whom she could turn in a time like this.

And didn't I have all kinds of reasons to avoid making that call? We didn't have much money, hardly enough to feed ourselves, much less five extra people. My husband was in school, and it was all we could do to scrape by each month on his GI benefits and his part-time music director's salary. Besides, where would everybody sleep in our tiny two-bedroom house? And she might not even accept my invitation.

I picked up the phone and dialed the store where Margaret worked. I began uncertainly, "Our pastor told me that you would have to be moving out this weekend. I just can't believe the landlady could be so heartless."

"Well, I don't understand why she's in such a hurry. There's no one waiting to rent it, but that's neither here nor there, I guess." Margaret talked matter-of-factly.

"I was just wondering if you might like to come stay with us for a while until you decide what to do?"

There was a long pause. Then, "Yes, I'd really appreciate that. I hate to impose, but I really don't have a choice. There's no one else." Her voice sounded relieved, but composed.

Later that day, she and the four children knocked on the door. My husband, my two-year-old son, and I greeted them as if they were a part of our family coming home from a year's absence. They responded accordingly, and that was the atmosphere that prevailed for the entire stay.

We made beds on the floor for all five children. Our son gladly gave up his bedroom for Margaret in exchange for the company of four "pajama buddies." Soon they were all bathed and dressed for bed. As I puttered around in the kitchen, putting away the dishes from our evening meal, I noticed a deafening silence, the kind one hears when five active children get quiet all at once.

I went to the kitchen door and peered curiously into the living room. There were Margaret and the children huddled together on the couch, the children listening to her as she read a Bible story. They were just finishing and each in turn was praying. They asked God to take care of their daddy while he was away and to take care of them the following day. Each added his thanks for being in our home and having such a fun night.

As I tiptoed back to the kitchen, those prayers were still ringing in my ears. How could she do it? Didn't she realize that her husband had just deserted her, that she didn't have a house, that her job couldn't support her?

We all got up the next morning a little earlier than usual to master the plan of feeding and dressing five children, one working mother, and a commuting student.

I suggested that Margaret deposit her seven-year-old, Tommy, at school on her way to work and let me keep the other three home for the day. She usually took the younger children to the tiny shop where she worked and let them play in the storage room in the rear. The owner didn't mind, and although it was hard on the children, it was the only solution. She couldn't pay a babysitter and buy groceries, too.

She agreed to let the children stay and play at our house. The day whizzed by, and the children were no trouble at all. It was amazing what three playmates could do for an only child.

So our days together continued. I kept the children at home; Margaret worked; Dan went to school. At night we watched television, read, or visited as if renewing an old friendship rather than beginning a new one.

By the end of the week, arrangements had been made by members of our church for Margaret and her children to move into a small house on the church property.

Our last night together Margaret told me how much she appreciated our hospitality and how much she had grown to love us. I assured her that we had been happy to have them and that I also had grown close to her. I wanted to say more, to pry into her thoughts, to ask what she planned to do, why she put up with her husband. But I did not.

Three days after Margaret moved out, I received a letter from her. She had somehow sensed all the questions I had withheld and felt that she was ready now to open her heart.

She admitted that her marriage had been disappointing and that she had wanted to dissolve it many times. But she had prayed that God would heal the marriage for the future of his children.

She thanked me for not asking the questions, for just being her friend and letting her think through her problems. She had needed the time to shore up her faith that God would work things out.

God did answer her prayers. Her husband returned some months later and sought medical help for his drinking problem. Today they have that dreamed-about, prayed-about home.

I have long since moved away from that city, but when I return, I never fail to visit Margaret. It is hard to remember one occasion when she didn't have someone who was weathering a crisis staying with her.

She and her husband opened their home to a newly married Mexican couple who moved to the city without a job. They provided shelter to a young mother and her small baby until her marital differences were reconciled.

This past Christmas as I stopped in to visit, she was leaving with her children to go shopping for gifts for an Indian family down the street. She is passing on to her children the joy of sharing.

Each time I see her reaching out to meet a new need, I ask myself how she can be so generous when she has so little herself. She explains it in that same simple, matter-of-fact way that is characteristic of the way she faces problems. God gives to us through other people, and we in turn are to pass it on.

Father Ritter Takes Kids Off the Market

His Covenant House is a place where young victims of Manhattan's sex industry can find sanctuary

By PAM ROBBINS

For Father Bruce Ritter, the Crucifixion is as real as the last kid who came through the door. The fifty-two-year-old* Franciscan priest is the founder and director of Covenant House, a New York City child-care agency which operates eight group homes and a 24-hour-a-day crisis center, called Under 21, for runaway children.

"In the suffering and despair of these children," Father Ritter says, "the Passion of Christ is relived every day on Eighth Avenue."

The sentiments might seem lofty when applied to these youngsters. And Father Ritter admits that they are not innocent: between eighty and ninety percent are engaged in prostitution and pornography. But they are drawn, he insists, not by lust or greed, but by fundamental needs for food and shelter.

Most are from the city and its surrounding areas. The rest come on rumbling buses from every part of the country. Police estimate that some 20,000 runaways flood New York at any given time. The majority are not off on a lark. They are fleeing from neglect, alcoholism, beatings, or sexual abuse. Even if they wanted to, most could not go home. So they are easy prey to those who merchandise children in the city's flourishing sex market.

For about a hundred youngsters a day, Father Ritter offers alternatives: crisis intervention, round-the-clock counseling, a meal, a bed,

---

*At the time of first publication of this article.

47

a shower, medical aid, referral, direction into programs—his own or others—to give them educational and job skills.

He does not do it alone. Besides the 250-member full-time staff, there are 150 volunteers and the Covenant House Community, a core group that is the spiritual life-force behind the work. These men and women commit one year or more to God and the children. They pray and fast and work, living an ascetical life which contrasts sharply to the self-indulgence rampant in Times Square.

Father Ritter tells the story of his community on an average of once a day, preaching forty-eight weekends of the year and innumerable week-days, anywhere he is invited. His favorite audience is high-school stu-dents. In that setting, there is a lot he can do: maybe stop a potential runaway, plant seeds in future community members, gain help for his particular children, and a halt to the sexual exploitation of all children.

This particular Monday morning, he is to speak to a general assembly of some 1,400 boys at Chaminade High School in Mineola, Long Island. Geographically, they do not live far from New York City; by all other measures they live light-years away. Many, the principal says, have never been downtown. In their ties and jackets, these college-bound boys seem the antithesis of Father Ritter's kids.

Chaminade, run by the Marianists, is well-built and maintained. The auditorium is impressive. The principal gives Father Ritter the kind of glowing introduction he dislikes, and the Franciscan steps out onto the well-lit stage. His stance is casual, his delivery conversational. It is his content that gradually takes hold of the audience.

"Within my Order, I was trained as an academician," he begins. "I taught for ten years, five at Manhattan College. My new assignment came about as a result of a direct confrontation between me and my students." He had preached a sermon about secularism and materialism, and ended with a question: "How long will it be before you sell out?" He had let the question linger, then turned back toward the altar, when a voice sang out: "Wait a minute, Bruce." The student then challenged him to lead, not by words, but by his own example.

"I wasn't doing anything really bad," Father Ritter reflects. "I was just leading a happy, middle-class, professional life, and loving it a lot." But he apologized to the students, and soon after that, he asked permission to rent an apartment on the East Side, an area dominated by the hard-drug scene, and minister to the poor.

In the building of seventy-five apartments where he lived, sixty were occupied by junkies who were certain he was an undercover narcotics officer disguised as a priest. Once convinced that he was a real priest, fear left them and "they began to redress the economic imbalance. They robbed me once a day, every day, for a month. They even took my black suit and collar, but they left my Franciscan habit and some Latin books.

"I became involved with kids quite by accident," he continues. "One night about two a.m., four boys and two girls, all under sixteen, knocked on my door and asked if they could sleep on the floor of my apartment. Feeling very put out and noble, I said yes. The next morning, the girls got up and cooked my breakfast—and burned it—and the boys got up and cleaned my apartment—and cased it," he joked. Someone slipped out and brought back four more youngsters. They were all homeless and had been living in an abandoned building until some junkies burned them out; they had refused the junkies' offer to pimp for them. They had found shelter briefly with a Yonkers couple, but the price had been to star in a pornographic film, so they had fled.

Father Ritter began making telephone calls to a score of social agencies. "I was going to wave my magic Roman collar and flash my credentials as a doctor in theology." With Catholic agencies, he was Father Ritter; with others, he was Dr. Ritter. It didn't help. The children were too old, too young, too sick, not sick enough, not reimbursable. What it boiled down to, he says, was that nobody in New York was operating a program for young prostitutes and hustlers.

At one point, he was warned that he was breaking the law by harboring and contributing to the delinquency of minors. He was advised that the smartest thing he could do was to have the children arrested. "I couldn't do that," he says. "So I kept them."

The original ten already were telling their friends and more youngsters were coming for help.

"I needed help and more space, so I went back to Manhattan College and told the kids who drove me off campus to come down and help me, and they did." So did students from throughout the area, including some from Mount St. Vincent, Marymount, and Fordham. He did whatever he could to feed the children, including driving a cab. "We began to run a completely illegal, unfunded child-care agency." They began taking over more and more apartments in the building. Since junkies are a fairly transient population, apartments became vacant often.

"Eventually," he says, "we had to become legal." In 1972, they received a charter as a nonprofit child-care agency. Franciscan Sisters joined him to work with the girls, and Covenant House began to grow as a bona fide operation. "Now we operate eight homes and a very special program in Times Square called Under 21.

"It's on the Minnesota Strip, ten blocks along Eighth Avenue with 100 sex-related businesses: massage parlors, topless bars, fleabag hotels, thousands of girls and young women, boys and men. It earns $1.5 billion a year.

"Ten years ago," he continues, "organized crime made the decision to get into sex in a very big way. The income to organized crime from sex surpasses that from gambling and loan sharking. It is second only to illicit drugs. It makes $5 to $10 billion per year."

He begins to tell the Chaminade students stories about the street, in vocabulary they have never heard from a priest—stories of pimps and hustlers and "johns," or customers, and a society that permits and even protects what he has called the "blatant, sick, savage destruction of children.

"The other morning, I went over to buy a newspaper and I saw a blond kid, about fifteen, in a doorway. I was dressed as a priest. Despite that, he gave me one of those long, unmistakable, propositioning looks. He was still there at five o'clock in the evening and the next morning."

Not long ago the priest had stopped to talk to a group of children. "The oldest was fifteen, and he was their pimp. He said, 'Which one do you want? You can have any one for $20.' I said I wasn't into that, and he said, 'Why don't you take this one? You'll like him. He's eleven.'

"I guess you would call my kids sinners. God knows they are certainly sinned against. But most of them are simply trying to survive. When you are fourteen or fifteen and it's cold and you're hungry and you have nothing to sell except yourself . . . you sell yourself. They face the cruelest possible dilemma."

At Under 21, which is never closed, "a lot of kids come in just for a chance to live. I can't tell you how many times a kid has said to me, 'Bruce, I'm not going to make it. The street is going to kill me. I'm going to die out there.'

"The other day, a seventeen-year-old girl came in. She was picked off near the bus terminal and held for ten days, drugged heavily, raped repeatedly—that's part of the conditioning process—and put out on the street to work. She had the courage to escape. She jumped out of her pimp's car and ran into the center.

"The same night, a ten-year-old boy came in, a cute kid, and he brought the trucks and cars his johns bought for him that day. He's too young to ask them for money, so they buy him toys instead. For some sick reason, the johns are beginning to want children. Children have become the merchandise in a sick and sad industry.

"The myth that prostitution is a victimless crime is the most bizarre myth ever foisted on a gullible public." Prostitution is seldom a simple business arrangement between a buyer and a seller. It is usually exploitation, it is often dangerous, it is sometimes fatal. Prostitutes, male and female, are viewed as property by their pimps. Children are no exception. If the boys at Chaminade remember nothing else, he hopes they will remember this.

He tells them about a pimp who makes his headquarters at the coffee shop across the street from Under 21. "Izzy has four girls, ages twelve to twenty-one. He has never been arrested. He probably never will be. It's a very well-protected industry." By way of example, there is Veronica. "Veronica, eleven years old, was arrested eight times for prostitution on Eighth Avenue. Never once did they check her age. Each time the judge looked at this child. And each time he gave her a $100 fine and her pimp, sitting in the courtroom, paid this small business expense and she was back on the street. Veronica was killed two weeks after she celebrated her twelfth birthday. She was thrown out of a tenth-story window on Times Square."

He recounts the story of a man convicted recently of running a giant "call-boy" operation. "You could call him and order a kid—5'10", blond, blue-eyed, swimmer's build. He would be delivered to your home or apartment. It would cost you $50 to $100, and you could use your charge card. If you ordered two or three, he'd give you a cut rate." Police found ample evidence in a raid, and the man pleaded guilty to a felony. He could have gotten seven years in jail, but the judge who tried him put him on probation. "He sold 400 kids a month over the phone, but he didn't spend a day in jail, and he now has a very fine job with the federal government.

"In our society, we have identified sex as entertainment," he continues. He believes this is a root cause of sexual exploitation.

Barely pausing for that message to sink in, Father Ritter switches subjects to talk about the Covenant House Community. "If you were twenty-one or twenty-two," he says, "I'd ask you to consider giving me a year of your life. I would give you room and board, $10 a week, insurance, and a chance to practice the spiritual and corporal works of mercy. You would pray three hours a day and fast at least once a week, on Thursdays.

"St. Francis told us we should never be ashamed to beg, but we should beg only for the love of God. So I'm begging you guys for the love of God to care about my kids, to pray for them, and to realize that they are your brothers and sisters. We are our brother's keepers."

The applause is strong and sustained, but the students' faces reveal little as they file out to return to their classes. Driving back into the city, Father Ritter wonders aloud what their reaction was. "It will be harder for those kids to talk about prostitution as a victimless crime," he muses.

"There's hope in those kids at Chaminade," he says. "Maybe one of them will become a lawyer or a judge. Maybe one of them will be a priest or a bishop—and he won't be afraid to speak out.

"One of the really dreadful things in our society is the acceptance of things like this. We almost encourage pornography—the degradation of an entire gender. I saw an ad recently with a beautiful young woman, dressed in black velvet. She was tied up and beaten black and blue, and she was smiling. I think that's obscene. And the fact that we use this to sell products . . ." he trails off, shaking his head.

"There has to be a change in public attitudes," he insists, if sexual exploitation is ever to end. Besides the long-range solutions, like strengthening families, changing attitudes, forming clear values, there are quick solutions available. "We could enforce the laws. They're not seriously prosecuted. A public outcry could turn the tide. The police do what they are told."

Father Ritter is tempted too often to anger. What keeps him going is hope. The main source of that hope is the people who form the Covenant House Community.

It began nearly three years ago when he first moved onto Eighth Avenue. "I was bankrupt and living there all alone. I thought about it a lot, prayed about it a lot, then I wrote a newsletter, inviting people to come and join me. And people began to do that."

He turns away many who wish to join. "I ask a person why he

wants to do it. If he says, 'I want to work with the kids and I want to do it for God,' I say no. Because the priorities are reversed.''

Members of the Community—who currently number about thirty —live in poverty and chastity and obey a simple community rule. There are no actual vows, rather an agreement, an understanding. They are deeply committed to three hours of prayer, two shared, one private, each day. "If you're not going to do that, then you can't stay," Father Ritter says.

While Religious can join, Father Ritter stresses that "the community is a lay community. I have forbidden any priest, Brother, or Sister to accept any leadership position within the community. My intervention is purely spiritual. I think it's absolutely true that laymen must exert leadership in the Church.''

Among the men and women in the community now are nurses, priests and Sisters, a computer programmer, a former bank employee, a statistician, a special education teacher, and a credit manager. They come from as far away as Canada, North Carolina, and Indiana. They span a wide age range, with the oldest admitting to being sixty-eight. They use whatever skills they have in working with the kids, but they are first of all a sign, living proof of a different set of values than the youngsters have known before. They exemplify the kind of no-strings love that Father Ritter preaches.

The work is bearing fruit. The figures, while lopsided, are another source of hope for Father Ritter. Of every 100 children who come into Under 21, maybe fifteen go back home, another fifteen are directed into programs, and the rest go back on the street. But Father Ritter sees the positive side of the coin. "We sent 1,200 kids home last year. That's a lot of kids. Another 1,200 to 1,500 are off the streets. We sent nine off to college this September—kids we picked off the street two or three years ago. We can give you a long list of kids who've made it against almost impossible odds. And we can give you a longer list of kids who haven't. But what is hope? Hope for our kids is that they begin to believe they have a future.''

No child is ever turned away at Under 21. "I used to turn them away, before I really knew what happens to a child on the street. Now I would fire anyone who turned one away. We may refuse shelter only if we know he has another place to go, with a secured bed.''

Another sign of hope is the sheer growth of Covenant House. "I didn't want the thing to become big. I knew it could, but this kind of thing is always strictly up to God. There's no way any of this could have happened if the Lord hadn't wanted it."

Apparently, the Lord did, since Covenant House is now a $6 million operation, with $4 million coming from private sources. The money is never easy to come by. It usually appears just as the creditors are nipping at Father Ritter's heels, but it comes.

The first giant step came for the organization in 1976, when the priest was approached to start a runaway shelter in Times Square. Starting from scratch, he found the Eighth Avenue building, elicited encouragement and a sum of money from Terence Cardinal Cooke, Archbishop of New York, and additional funds from his own Franciscan Order and the Charles Culpepper Foundation. Under 21 was born, and Father has stayed slightly ahead of insolvency ever since.

The second giant step came in December, 1979, when Covenant House opened expanded headquarters at 460 West 41st Street in a complex of three buildings which formerly housed a drug rehabilitation program. Father Ritter was able to lease the space from the state for one dollar a year for ten years, with the understanding that he would do any renovations.

The new facility includes more sleeping space for youngsters—with beds instead of sleeping mats—and better office space. It also includes a medical clinic staffed by one full-time physician and one full-time nurse, plus volunteer personnel. It is a dream come true for him, since most of his children have no access to health care. His next big thrust will be toward educational and vocational programs.

Father Ritter has a life insurance policy which will assure that Covenant House can carry on without him. Meanwhile he continues his work, wishing every day that he were still teaching medieval studies at Manhattan College.

Those who would like to help can do a number of things. They can pray, first of all. They can press for legislation and enforcement of laws against prostitution and pornography. They can work to strengthen the family, so that one million children won't leave home each year. They can give their time to Covenant House. They can send food, clothing, toilet articles, and money. "We are always broke," he says simply.

Samaritan to the Sewer Rats

*Tony Messineo brings food, clothing, and a sympathetic
ear to drifters on the St. Louis riverfront*

By WILLIAM McSHANE

Tony Messineo doesn't care much for the term "sewer rats" when
talking about his personal apostolate down by the Mississippi river.
Sewer rats, or river rats, are popular names for people who hang around
the river and the pipes that empty into it. "But these are human beings
down there," Messineo said.

"We have right here in St. Louis a group that is not even acknowl-
edged," he continued. "Some consider them the lowest of low. Ba-
sically, they are people who have divorced themselves from the human
race. They couldn't cope and they're out.

"Among them we don't have anything as glamorous as an ex-judge,
an ex-lawyer, a fallen doctor. I do know of one who is an ex-insurance
salesman. There are many men, but some women, too, up and down
the river front living around the sewers that empty into the river. Some
even go into the pipes because it's warmer there, especially in winter."

Messineo came across this group of people several years ago by
accident and began wondering who was helping them out. He discovered
that no one was.

"Many organized groups would not even acknowledge them," he
said. "I talked to several police officers who said, 'Yes, but . . .' They
just don't want to get mixed up with them. All I try to do is feed them
when I can, clothe them when I can. But I can't spend all my time
down there."

So, without the help of organizations, he and several others make
frequent trips to the river front to do what they can for society's dropouts.
Messineo and his helpers get clothes from their families and friends.

Several restaurants save leftovers for him, and on Saturdays he goes to Soulard Market to pick up things that have been discarded.

"I consider myself a beggar for this food, but that's all I will be. I won't beg for money, no way I'll get mixed up in that," he added.

Why, in fact, get involved at all?

"Years ago, I decided to do something with my life," he related. "After a couple of retreats and a talk with my spiritual advisor, I made a commitment to Jesus Christ and to Our Lady of Mount Carmel.

"I try to live as close as I can to a monastic life while living in this world. What it all boils down to is that we are placed on earth to know, love and serve God in this world, and be happy with Him in the next."

Then, a few years ago, Messineo read an ad in a national weekly for the Association of Mary Immaculate, a lay religious Community headquartered in Jacksonville, Florida, which invited "single, mature men and women to serve the Lord through their own profession and lifestyle, by means of private vows." Messineo, already fulfilling the requirements, joined, and has since made his private vows.

Now fifty-six, he finds time for both his job as kitchen manager at St. John's Mercy Medical Center and his river-front mission. After meeting his own needs, he uses his earnings to help support his apostolate. "God gives to me, I give to them."

His regular visits to the river area began several years ago, he recalled. "I saw a guy lying near the railroad tracks. I watched for a while and actually thought he was dead, until I got closer and realized he was in a stupor.

"We talked, very guardedly, and then we were joined by somebody else from down there. And then I asked myself, 'Why are these people living like this?' They're relatively young, not in the senior citizens age group. Well, scratch the surface and you'll find out why: they can't cope.

"Time stands still for these people," he explained. "No income tax deadlines to meet, no bills to pay. They don't worry about anything. It's a transient group, especially among the younger ones. And with the warmer weather there are more teenagers, who often turn to violence or anything else to make a buck.

"The older ones just seem to hang around, vegetating. They hide behind their grain alcohol, mixed with a quart of boiling water. They get by. Then, too, after a while, their lamps go out. Know what I mean?''

Messineo has gotten close to several of the older people. He lets them choose the topics for discussion. ''The weather is always a good opening,'' he noted. ''They're not interested in politics. My usual is, 'What are you going to do if it snows? Gets too hot? Have you eaten lately?' They will volunteer things, but if you press them you've lost them. Keep quiet, don't pump them is the best approach.

''They seldom bring up the subject of religion because that means they are getting close to coming back to the human race. They begin to talk about values then.''

On Marian Day several months ago Messineo and two of his helpers recited the Rosary in one of the sewers. ''It started out with three of us and three of them. Well, word got around and by the time we finished there were eighteen of us in that sewer. Our seminarian intoned *Salve Regina* and before we knew it these people were singing Latin right along with us. Some say there is no God, but no matter where people hide He finds them.

''I feel that only in God's own good time will we really see anything for them down there. Right now, we are only buying time, feeding the bodies, getting them to rejoin the human race. But once they regain a little dignity they will see the goodness of God. Until they shape up they won't see anything. You can't see anything on an empty stomach or an empty head. Right now the heads are so full of grain alcohol that it's going to be impossible.

''If you preach to them, all you are going to see is their dust. And let me tell you, there are very few places you can preach about them. They're the unloved, unwelcomed, unaccepted, the kind that bring a 'Don't look at them, they'll go away' reaction.''

He added, however, that his work could not be done ''if it wasn't for the prayers of other people, the nuns who pray for me and this type of work. It is impossible to do this kind of work yourself. You have to have the spiritual support.''

Helping Each Other in the Great Depression

Christian brotherhood has always been the key to surviving hard times

By DOROTHY DAY

These days one hears a lot of talk comparing the present hard times with the Great Depression of the '30's. In the '30's, there was not a radio in every home and a transistor in every pocket to remind us hourly of all the bad news. But we still realized then that we were all in the same boat. And somehow, as in times of earthquake and flood, everyone's disaster was no one's disaster. There was no sense of personal failure, no guilt to make the load heavier. And many began to see that they could not only help themselves, but also help each other.

Even while people were presenting demands, demonstrating in front of Home Relief offices, and staging marches on City Hall and on Washington, they were doing a lot on their own.

The *Catholic Worker*, for example, a penny-a-copy paper of which I am the publisher, began in 1933 in the kitchen of my own apartment on New York's lower East Side. My younger brother helped me with layout and headlines, and we sold the papers ourselves in the streets.

One of our helpers, a college graduate, slept in Central Park every night, was arrested every morning, jailed for the day, then released to go back to the park or railroad station. But he wrote stories about his experiences, which helped increase the circulation of the paper. He much preferred, of course, to write articles on liturgy and sociology.

Another helper lived in a basement apartment, rent-free, with his wife and two babies, in return for helping a maintenance man carry out the ashes and the garbage each day. There was a broken dumb-waiter in this six-story building, so the tenants threw their garbage down the shaft, and the man had to dig it out. It was a gruesome task: rats kept leaping out of the shaft where they had been feasting on the garbage.

I lived in an adjoining basement apartment. We had heat and hot water, but my little daughter slept in a crib that had to be screened because the rats were so numerous. I soon moved to a heatless apartment on 15th Street. In the back were gardens of flowers and little fruit trees. One could heat by gas oven, but that made the bills high.

To me, the most interesting housing, and a splendid example of people banding together in distress, was the "jungle" at the foot of East 10th Street, where the East Side Drive is now. Its residents would pick up old furniture and bits of lumber on the street and construct little villages like those one sees in Tijuana today. I remember writing a sarcastic story about a rich man who would bring fresh vegetables from his country home to the men in the jungle. I'm sorry now for my sarcasm. God bless the man's kind heart and the courage it took to do these deeds. Perhaps he had a boyish, romantic yearning for such a life, which most men of his position think of as irresponsible. Sometimes I think the hardest thing the poor and the destitute have to bear is the ready judgment passed on them for not managing better.

Our *Catholic Worker* grew, and I received many invitations to speak at Catholic schools and colleges around the country. I was delighted to find that such jungles had sprung up all over. In the South, in the Northwest, wherever I traveled, I found them.

In our paper we looked forward to what we called the "personalist and communitarian revolution," a nonviolent social change inspired by the love of God, which we could show only by love of our brothers. This philosophy resulted in our opening "houses of hospitality." A young woman who had been sleeping nights in the subway told us bitterly, "You write about hospices; why don't you start one?"

What could we do? One of our members and I walked down the street and found an apartment near Stuyvesant Park. There were six rooms with a bath and hot water. We scraped and begged enough for the first month's rent. We called up and had the gas and electricity turned on.

To me, the most important aspect of the Depression was that we were left alone, not interfered with by city and state agencies in these hospices of ours.

We telephoned the parish priest and asked him if he knew any charitable parishioners who would contribute sheets, towels, blankets, and perhaps some beds or cots. Before nightfall the rooms were swept, two beds set up, a few plates, pots, and cutlery provided, and two women were "sleeping in" instead of riding the subways.

Some of the men complained that we were neglecting them, so we found an empty house in back of St. Brigid's Church on Tompkins Square. The priest there said it had been left to the church, and of course we could use it, but he was as broke as we were. At least the men had a roof over their heads.

Our next move was to a brownstone near the waterfront in Greenwich Village. A young priest at St. Veronica's Church begged us to take it over. He wanted us to start a parish credit union and a maternity guild, as a way of helping poor families.

After a year, we made another move. One of our readers, a devout woman, told us that she owned an empty house which could be ours if we wished to clean it up. This was in 1935. A big East Coast seamen's strike had begun in May, and six of the men had come and asked us for lodging. So they got busy and swabbed the decks, as it were, and helped us with the moving.

We were like a large family in that house. There were twenty rooms, and lots of fireplaces, so we had beautiful fires, with coal brought in by our Italian neighbors. Poorer folks than we burned wood salvaged from crates and boxes. Later, we had hot water. Many of the Italian families helped us with food, clothing, and furniture. We lived in this home of ours, which we called St. Joseph's House, for fifteen years, till long after the Depression.

For food, there were cans of what we called home-relief beef. When neighbors, tired of this diet, came to exchange a half-dozen cans for some clothes or blankets, we were only too happy to accept. Other surplus commodities were plentiful, especially corn meal for mush or corn bread. Many times we scrounged around the markets for the outer leaves of lettuce and cabbage for a soup, and one of our specialties was mashed potatoes with mushroom gravy, the mushrooms too blackened to be sold on the market and so given to us.

Early issues of the *Catholic Worker* told of our adventures in handling evictions in our city neighborhood. We begged money for rent, and then a troop of us would find an apartment for $12 or $15 a month and move the family ourselves by pushcarts. Even our neighbors' children helped us, carrying washboards, ironing boards, pails or pans and cutlery, clothes and pillows.

I tell these details to point out all the small things accomplished *by the people themselves*. They were straws in the wind, but they need to be remembered.

The Depression of the '30's ended with the Second World War. There was full employment, a great growth in job opportunities, increased incomes, and new social legislation enacted.

But now we have another depression, complicated by inflation. Programs like Medicaid and Medicare and Social Security are supposed to take care of unemployment and poverty, but rents have skyrocketed. Today, when we try to house a family in an emergency, two months' rent is required in advance, and a large deposit for gas and electricity, not to speak of finding the simplest equipment or furnishings.

Times are indeed hard. But I see hopeful signs that people are again realizing, as they did in the '30's, that they can do something to help themselves and each other. Among the young, especially, there are growing communities on the land, and not just the "communes" which are so widely publicized.

Where land is cheap, you will find young married couples forming land trusts with others around them, from California to New England. There is food to be grown on the land, and timber to build and heat with. And there are heroic battles to be fought with those who threaten our resources and spoil our countryside with strip mining.

Perhaps backyard gardens will be popular again, as they were in wartime, and trees will be planted again. A *Catholic Worker* hospice in San Francisco has made a little paradise of a vacant lot a block from its headquarters. The real estate man lets them use it until it is sold; then they will find another.

Ideas like these, springing up in this current depression, may be called simplistic, but the new generation meeting this crisis is not afraid of words. They know that to meet the depression of the '70's, we must simplify our needs, and realize that we ourselves—each of us—can do a little. And that a little here and there amounts to much.

St. Jude's Hospital, St. Mary's Parish

One helps Danny Thomas's children, the other helps their parents

By ROBERT R. HOLTON

St. Mary's Church in downtown Memphis is a haven for people in deep distress. Over the last six years about fifty members of the congregation have "adopted" cancer-stricken children and their families who have come to the world-famous St. Jude Children's Research Hospital founded by entertainer Danny Thomas.

St. Mary's, like many other parishes in center cities, relies on Catholics from the suburbs to support it, thereby creating an economically, educationally, and culturally mixed congregation.

"Actually, these people come from all walks of life," says pastor Father Brian Szorady. "For the most part, the Good Samaritans who reach out to the St. Jude families have very little in common with each other except for a burning desire to act out the Gospel of Jesus Christ by trying to make life a little bit more bearable for these distraught parents and their sick kids."

The insertion of these critically ill children and their kin into the mainstream of the St. Mary's "family" usually begins when they come to attend Mass or to pray for a very special intention in the church's Lady of Lourdes grotto.

They stand out in the crowd, these sad-eyed, nervous visitors from faraway places. There are the children themselves, their heads marred by patches of baldness, their complexions often a toneless alabaster, their wrists and ankles twig-thin, their tiny frames barely fleshed. Many times they are in wheelchairs.

Usually their mothers accompany them to the church. Sometimes a father will be able to break away from his job in a distant city long enough to visit with them for a weekend, but mostly the visitors are just the mother and the ailing child whose cancer has been diagnosed as catastrophic, making him eligible for the free treatment at St. Jude Hospital. The hospital also pays the transportation cost for the child and one adult, and picks up the bill for a hotel room a few blocks from the hospital and just across the street from St. Mary's Church.

The initial stay in Memphis is usually about three weeks, while the patient's condition is pinpointed and treatment is begun. After the first phase, the child normally returns at prescribed intervals for continuing treatment.

The emotional and physical strain of the Memphis visits is intensified for patient and parent alike by the strange surroundings and the separation from home and family. Very often the child is too ill from the combination of disease and chemotherapy even to be taken to the hotel dining room for meals. But if the child can walk or can endure an hour or more sitting up in a wheelchair, St. Mary's Catholic Church shines like a beacon just across the street.

"The minute they step into the church they are spotted by our parishioners," says Father Brian. "There's no magic formula and we have no prepared spiel. When you spot them, you walk up to them and you say what comes to your mind. I guess the Holy Spirit really does the talking through our parishioners."

Mary Wrigley, who with her husband has developed close associations with more St. Jude families over the years than anyone else in the parish, explains the initial meeting this way:

"You see them in the back of the church and you walk up and say who you are. Sometimes you say where you work or what you do. It sort of breaks the ice. Then you mention that you don't have anything to do for the next couple of hours and you offer to take them to the coffee shop and buy them a cup of coffee or a soda. No mention is made of illness. But soon, the parents will say how long they've been in the city and then blurt out why they are here."

After the first meeting, Mrs. Wrigley says, arrangements are made for future get-togethers. Lunches and dinners soon follow up as the relationships begin to take hold and grow.

"It's no big deal," she insists. "All we're really doing here is trying the best way we can to live the Gospel. We're really fortunate to be given these golden opportunities to help other people."

Father Brian began visiting St. Jude patients as a part-time Catholic chaplain in 1971 when he was an associate pastor at St. Mary's. In 1974, he was named administrator of the downtown parish and Catholic chaplain at the hospital. Since then, about fifty members of the parish have gotten involved with St. Jude patients and their families.

Father Brian says he oversees the contacts between his parishioners and the St. Jude families. "I make certain that the people who establish these relationships are strong enough—emotionally and in other ways —to handle them," he says. "I also must make sure that the parishioner knows it is not just a matter of inviting someone home to dinner for an afternoon of family living and then dropping them cold. You have to be consistent and follow up, or you can do more harm than good. The first invitation is just the beginning."

One mother of a fifteen-year-old suffering with leukemia says she doubts that she could handle the emotional strain without the relationships she has had with Father Brian and the St. Mary's parishioners.

"That's not a parish there at St. Mary's," the mother says. "That's one big, happy, compassionate and considerate family that just happens to meet to worship together at the same place."

She likens her relationships with the parishioners to "being home in Indiana and having my own family and longtime friends with me when the going gets rough."

Another mother whose youngster is under treatment at St. Jude Hospital said she doubts she could have endured the "virtual house arrest of living day after day in a hotel room.

"And if it wasn't for the St. Mary's crowd, that's exactly what life would be for me—one visit a day to the hospital with my child and then back to pacing the floor for hours in the hotel room, talking to myself while my sick youngster slept," she says. "Instead of that, St. Mary's people have expanded my world into their homes and into their family atmospheres. You have no idea how comforting that is at a time like this when you feel so completely powerless and at everyone's mercy."

"We have hundreds of cards and letters from people taken in by parishioners during their visits here to St. Jude's," says Father Brian. "Some of the letters are from parents of kids who made it and are in long-term remission from their diseases. Others, of course, are from parents of kids who just didn't make it."

Not since the St. Mary – St. Jude relationship began has a single patient drawn more attention than Billy Baker, a seven-year-old leukemia victim. For four years before the disease claimed his life, Billy said he had been having regular visits from God.

"He (God) was the first one to tell me that I had a real bad disease," Billy told a newspaper reporter. "But God said not to worry because everything was going to be all right."

Weighing his words and speaking in a steady voice, with the vocabulary of a person many years his senior, Billy had said, "That news from God sitting on my bed shocked me for a minute. But God told me death is just like leaving. He said He's got a room ready for me. I have to leave my family but He said they will come up later."

Billy's engaging story found its way into newspapers across the nation.

"It's been almost a year and I'm still not over Billy's death," says Father Brian. "I'm a Hungarian-Irishman and highly emotional. And Billy really got to me. He used to serve Mass for me. In the beginning the little guy would hold the Mass book up in his outstretched arms for me to read. As time went on and he got weaker, he'd rest it on the top of his head. Towards the end, he would just sit there or kneel with me during Mass. He got to me more than any of the rest. I still have his little teddy bear on a bookshelf in my office."

Doctors at St. Jude Hospital say that by treating Billy as they did, they added about four years to his life, reports Father Brian. "And the day Billy died, his mother said the four years St. Jude gave to Billy were the happiest she had ever had with him."

"That little fellow left a lot behind for all of us to feed on," says one elderly St. Mary's parishioner. "He was suffering a lot, we know now. But he always had a smile and something kind and cute to say."

An autopsy on Billy's body, one source says, gave St. Jude researchers answers to some nagging questions about how his type of cancer can best be treated. "That," says Father Brian, "and the lessons he taught us about how to have faith in God and suffer silently, are part of the Billy Baker legacy.''

The patient benefits from the St. Mary – St. Jude relationships are not overlooked by the crack professional staff in the hospital.

Dr. Richard Wilber, a thirty-two-year-old research associate in pediatric infectious disease control at the hospital, says, ''The interaction between the patients and their parents and the parishioners makes our job here a great deal easier.''

''It is much more difficult for us if the parents, particularly the mothers who are with the children the most, are emotionally devastated,'' says Dr. Wilber, a married father of two children who is a candidate for the permanent diaconate.

''If the mother is too emotionally upset, she will not be able to make and pass on to us her best day-to-day observations of the child's behavior and reactions to treatment. These reactions are extremely important to the doctor in plotting the treatment program. Also, bringing these people into genuine family relationships in a real home atmosphere increases the quality of life for the parent as well as the patient.

''There is no one, from the top administrators on down at the hospital, who does not feel deep gratitude to the people of St. Mary's for what they are doing.''

Looking back over the years the program has been in operation, Father Brian still is uncertain how it all began.

''Oh, for me as a priest, it was a natural enough thing,'' he says. ''I was ordained to ministry and I was called to St. Jude's to do my thing. But these men and women of the parish—and that includes people of all ages—just sort of fell into this relationship without any of us ever realizing that it was happening.''

He says he has never had a formal meeting about the program.

''The only meetings we have had are meetings at which we discussed the Gospel and prayed,'' he emphasizes. ''I never once programmed these people. It all just sort of happened.''

''As much as possible we bring the visitors into our complete family round of activities,'' Mrs. Wrigley points out. ''We snack at the kitchen table rather than set a formal table in the dining room. We play cards together or watch television together. Some of the St. Mary's people will have their grandchildren in to play with the little patients. Or, if they are young enough, they'll have their own youngsters play with the patients. We have cookouts in the backyard and we often go to one of the parks with a picnic lunch. The trick is to do together the very same things you do with your own family.''

Mrs. Wrigley and her trucking-firm executive husband have worked with about a dozen patients and their families. Both were at the bedsides of four youngsters when they died.

"When the end draws near, the parents of the children usually call their adopted families or me and ask that they be there when death comes," Father Brian says. "No one wants to die alone and most people want someone else with them when their loved one dies. It helps.''

Usually those in the St. Mary program vow after one of the children dies that they will not open themselves to such a trauma again.

"But we always come back for more," says one couple. "We feel at first we can't do it. But then we realize that we have an obligation and we get all caught up again.''

Mrs. Jack Gaia says she and her husband became involved with a St. Jude family because of her love for golf.

"I was leaving church after a weekday Mass in 1977, and Father Brian said something in a joking way about my being headed for the golf course," she recalls. "I agreed that I was and a cute little boy about twelve years old heard me say it. He came over to me and asked if he could play golf with me sometime.''

Mrs. Gaia agreed and they set a date and went to the golf course a few days later.

"In the meantime, I had learned that he was a leukemia patient at St. Jude's and was from Georgia and here with his mother for treatment. We went golfing and became fast friends. I practically lived with the family from October 1977 until he died in January of 1978.''

When the boy died, Mrs. Gaia and her husband attended the funeral.

"Then we took up with another little boy named Joe, from Michigan," she explains. "He died two months later. I was at their bedsides when both of the youngsters died. The mothers and fathers had asked me to come. We were that close.''

All of the men and women in the program express deep religious convictions and maintain that without them they never would be able to participate in such a program.

"You've got to be convinced in your heart that God has a reason for taking these innocent young people,'' says Mrs. Wrigley. ''You have to have faith that there is a hereafter. Without that, no one could handle this duty.''

In his eulogy at Billy Baker's funeral, perhaps Father Brian summed it up best:

''Billy Baker, a little boy, a patient, a saint. Billy Baker, all boy and all normal, with dirty little fingernails and scuffed-up shoes. Billy Baker, who suffered more than he told us about.

''Billy Baker, take care of us. You gave up your body so that other children may live. Give us your strength that we might lead more meaningful lives. Take away our bitterness and our anger, Billy Baker.''

Leprosy Is a
Disease of the Heart

*In my clinical tour through the horrors of Bombay, had I
committed the worst sin of a physician?*

By RALPH CRAWSHAW, M.D.*

Seen through the rain, the hospital sat behind its dilapidated walls like some inundated ruin. I passed a wavering file of patients, some clutching children, some on crutches, some with torn pieces of plastic held over their bent cramped bodies, like a line of fiddler crabs limping and scurrying through the hospital's gate.

I had been invited by Dr. Shubhada Pandya to join her here at the Acworth Leprosy Hospital, Bombay, India. Inside the scarred two-story building, she greeted me. She is a youngish woman, slim in her white coat, who obviously does not spend afternons over tea and pastry. Her penetrating gaze conveys a gentleness continually challenged by the violence of intransigent disease. From her glowing, dark eyes to her sandaled feet she is a picture of focused intensity.

"You must understand from the beginning," she explained in the clipped accent of Indian English, "that this disease is a socioeconomic one. Leprosy is on the increase in this country. Should anyone tell you that it will be eliminated by the year 2000, poppycock! Our hospital treats 5,000 cases a year, and each day we see 250 new patients, even though they may have been diagnosed elsewhere. All patients get treatment. In fact, the necessary drugs can be supplied for a patient in adequate doses at a cost of only fifty cents per year. However, they must be taken for a lifetime, and patient compliance here, as the world over, is a sometimes thing."

*The author is a Portland, Oregon, physician.

We made our way out a back door onto a sheltering veranda where several men and boys were busy hammering and sawing, making chairs and desks. Dr. Pandya explained that although they were not economically competitive, since it was a sheltered workshop, the state had agreed to buy the furniture made by patients with leprosy. However, as in all things connected with leprosy, arrangements are never easy. She had been unable to find anyone in the city of Bombay to supervise these young men, who in turn were reluctant to learn, since patients could make more in the trades that already support eighty percent of Bombay's patients with leprosy: prostitution and bootlegging. Only a few dedicated patients stay long enough to become carpenters.

The rain had let up, so we stepped from beneath the dripping veranda for Dr. Pandya to demonstrate the symptomatology of the young men in better light. "This lad has a rash over his lower arm and hand which could easily pass as impetigo, and yet he is in the infectious state. He has responded well to medication and if he sticks with it, the rash will subside and he will probably suffer no serious complications. Probably, that is, but only if he sticks with the medication and cares for himself. Remember, this is a socioeconomic disease. Once he is diagnosed as a leper he is fired from his job. He is continually tempted to conceal his illness, both from his employer and himself, simply to make enough to eat."

She directed my attention to an older man. "Here, look at the nodules around the ears. These are like the tubercles of tuberculosis, each loaded with Hansen's bacteria. With adequate treatment this will subside. We seldom see what was once the characteristic leonine face. Disfigurements are not as prevalent as they used to be, though the disease is on the increase.

"Here is a claw hand," and she pointed out a man holding a chisel between two stumps of hands. "The ulnar nerve has been attacked. Notice how difficult it is for him to work, yet he works. The most important part of our work—and it seems like we never can accomplish it—is to have the patient learn to protect himself. He must not pick up anything hot. He must wear special shoes. But telling a patient to get special shoes is like telling him to buy a Rolls-Royce. The disease causes the loss of pain fiber. Stepping on a nail, cutting a foot, or burning a finger goes unnoticed until a secondary infection produces the ulcers you smell when you enter the hospital."

She called over an older man with leonine features. "Zemil has worked here for three years and is helping us teach carpentry. You see his nose has collapsed. The cartilage is gone. Incidentally, most of the transmission of leprosy is through the nose."

I asked her if she was not afraid of leprosy for herself. There was no question in my mind but that I was afraid of leprosy for me. I hesitated to touch a patient or shake any hands even when proffered out of clean, white coats.

She answered, "No, I know I've had leprosy. It's like tuberculosis. Most of us have had tuberculosis as a primary tuberculosis focus. The same is true of leprosy, a primary eruption. It is a matter of immunology, and so much of that is nutrition and as I say, this is a socioeconomic disease. It happens to the rich as well as the poor, but it happens mostly to the poor, and it will disfigure and destroy the poor who cannot protect themselves properly. Shoes, clothing, cleanliness, and food. Oh yes, I'm quite sure I've had leprosy."

We moved back to a room where female patients were being trained as seamstresses. Dr. Pandya continued, "You see, if we can get our women to make any sum of money, just the least, they will immediately be taken back by their families. However, when they have no money to contribute to their families, they are forever outcasts. It really makes little difference whether they are lepers or not. It's whether they are adding to the family's food."

We made our way on to the treatment clinic up a back stairway, through a crowded corridor—dark except for a lone neon tube flickering against the ceiling. In the doorway of the long room, a knot of people had formed about a young doctor who was lecturing a dark-skinned, apathetic, youngish man. It was more an argument than a consultation. After a perfunctory introduction, the doctor turned back to the patient, explaining to me over his shoulder that the man had just been diagnosed as having Hansen's disease.

"Look." She pointed to the butterflylike configuration of inflamed skin shaded ever so lightly redder than the rest of the man's face, but distinct once pointed out. "He is telling me that he doesn't want to come back to be treated, and he is in the infectious stage. He says that if he takes the treatment his employer will find out and he will no longer be able to support himself and his family. He has to protect his job, but his disease is sure to spread, not only to him but to his children. What is there to do? How loud should I shout at him to tell him that he has to come back?''

As though in relief to the pervasive despair, Dr. Pandya drew in a father and daughter for me to see. The short gray-haired father, in a Western three-piece suit and tie, had obviously come on important business. His daughter, probably sixteen years old, in a shimmering blue sari, stood sullenly beside him. He was elated, as Dr. Pandya explained: "He thought his daughter had leprosy. See, this discoloration around the mouth, a loss of pigment, we see that at times, and I know it's not leprosy, and I told him so but he is having trouble believing. Understand that in this country marriages are arranged, and if the woman is damaged—and there is no doubt that leprosy is a damage—it will be very difficult for her father to marry her off. You can see, he has trouble believing that such good fortune could happen to him, that his daughter does not have leprosy.''

The man's face was alternately lighting with smiles and darkening with frowns as he looked first to one and then another doctor, hoping that each and all would concur with him in beating down the fear that his beautiful daughter was damaged property.

"Come and see our dressing station," suggested Dr. Pandya, and we elbowed our way into the center of the long room where a wall of half-open jalousies did nothing to relieve the stench of putrid flesh. Rows of disfigured patients seated on the long benches proclaimed the final stages of leprosy: arms missing, faces askew, hands clawed, infected stumps. The floor was a litter of blood-soaked gauze and mud. "They are not infectious, probably, but they have lost most sensation in their bodies and secondary infection is killing them all," she remarked.

Leading me downstairs and back to the entrance, Dr. Pandya explained, "Now, I'll turn you over to Dr. Ganapati who will take you into the field." As she spoke, an attendant rushed up with a note that caused her face to light up. "See, we are having some effect. Here is a referral from a doctor. For so long doctors have not even referred patients to us for treatment for leprosy," and then with a sobering second thought, "but perhaps it is that some doctors are willing to recognize leprosy now simply to rid their practice of lepers.''

* * *

Dr. Ganapati proved to be an unprepossessing, middle-aged man, with a short-sleeved white shirt open at the neck, neat slacks, thick horn-rimmed glasses, receding hairline, and gray about the temples. As we lurched along, he shouted over the unmuffled roar of our van that we were headed for the Dharavi slums, where the Bombay Leprosy Project had one of its stations in case detection, treatment, and public education. Today, we were delivering drugs and other supplies to the Dharavi middle school, where the principal had generously allowed the project to undertake a health survey.

Before we reached the turn-off, he explained that this slum was reputed to be one of the worst. The inhabitants lived in degradation, eating, sleeping, defecating, urinating, and copulating in the open. The dangers for children are fierce.

Unexpectedly, we veered off the viaduct onto a side road that became a byway straggling down to a lane, which contracted to a passageway barely wide enough to allow our van to squeeze through. Up close, poverty is a gigantic, socially propelled slime mold, without form, yet an inexorable force that defiles everything it touches. Poverty's essence is trash, and with the exception of a very few faces lighted with dignity despite a life of suffering, everything else in the slum was broken, torn, besmirched, mismatched, or worn. There were pieces of glass, rusted cans, piles of offal, garbage, shattered barrels, crushed plastic bottles. There were sickly chickens, thin pigs looking to eat the chickens, small, weak children, shreds of human beings, yet beating the pigs with sticks. Everywhere a trash of expressions: scowls, threatening stares, disgust, and surprised hostility at the presence of an invading European.

Slowly we made our way to the school, which could be heard before it was seen, since this one massive building in the Dharavi was filled to bursting with screaming students. (School attendance is discouraged. Since there are more children than seats, a high dropout rate—which might better be called a forceout rate—is necessary.) It was filled to overflowing with a trash of discordant noise.

The Leprosy Project's station was an airless room on the school's third floor. The windows were closed to lessen the piercing racket of the classes. The doctor gave me a close view of the project, complete with slides—again, photographs of leprosy and, inadvertently, a picture of a physician who is fighting leprosy. When one slide announced, "Leprosy can be cured," I did not confront the doctor with my doubts.

The doctor accentuated repeatedly the paradox of Hansen's disease: the undamaged, infectious nose disseminates, while the disfigured but noninfectious face repels. The carrier easily passes in society, while the burned-out, noninfectious patient causes people to shrink. Slide after slide, some showing how symptoms can be contained, some showing how prevention can work; statistics showing how the sheer mass of people makes contagion inevitable. It is madness to think the disease can be eliminated by the year 2000. If I needed convincing, which I did not, the slide showing the yearly incidence of new cases among children in this school—fifty-five a year—was the clincher.

When our lecture ended, we made our way out of the school, and our talk turned to the role of the medical profession in fighting leprosy. Dr. Ganapati's voice, although not penetrating, had a clarity of understated conviction that carried through rather than over the turmoil. "I do not hold it against medical students who seek to become surgeons. A bright student does not take long to see where the profession gives recognition, and to know that with the recognition goes freedom from the insecurity of living on state budgets which are always endangered by political whim. No, I can understand why medical students are not attracted to working with a disease that lacks glamor and continually threatens your own health."

His explanation continued as our bus moved out of the Dharavi and into the wider streets of Bombay, but my eyes were open to a different matter, for when the bus stopped at an intersection, or a traffic light, and I saw those countless hands shoved in through the half-open window—the begging hands of children and adults, all imploring money—I was now alert to the leper's claw, the subtle rash of Hansen's disease, and the meaning of stumps for fingers. Despite this distraction, I listened closely to the doctor, trying hard to understand his forgiveness of medical students, hoping it included traveling physicians such as myself.

The van eventually wended its way back to my five-star hotel. I gratefully thanked my guide and the driver, who cheerfully waved me up the marble steps as the doorman let me into my immaculate, air-conditioned palace. I turned to wave back only to see them submerging into the flow of traffic milling about the "Gateway of India." I went to my room, where I removed my shoes before entering. Balancing my camera carefully on the edge of the bathroom sink, I stripped naked, rolled all my clothes into a tight bundle, placed them in a plastic laundry bag, and plunged beneath a hot soapy shower, where I remained for thirty minutes.

Once my body was cleansed as only a scrubbing with soap and hot water can do, I slipped into a fresh robe and retired to the sitting room of my suite. In the silence of the dark room, I slumped into a large chair, chin on chest, arms splayed, staring straight ahead into the cool shaded dimness, the picture of a defeated Roman general sorting through a lost campaign. All I had were thoughts, thoughts to be arranged and rearranged, until at last the diagnosis of leprosy, that grim socioeconomic disease, would make sense to me.

What did I think? I thought my eye sharp enough to see the lesions, the loss of pigment, the fine macular quality of the infected skin, the nodules around the ears that would never again go unrecognized by me. But those were clinician's thoughts. What did I think? I thought it curious that there is no physical pain connected with this disease. There is no squeezing chill or overbearing fever as in malaria; just the faintest touch—so easily denied—of dread death. Diabolically, leprosy preserves the illusion of health by destroying the pain fibers that lead to the brain. So the pain of leprosy originates in the eyes of the beholder, and becomes pain for the patient as he is shunned and ostracized, as he loses the humanness he once possessed. The pain of leprosy is not inflicted by the bacillus but by the leper's fellow man. And I did not know what to make of this.

A terrible equation appeared before my eyes. If I am a human being and patients with leprosy are human beings, we are of the same flesh; therefore some part of me is a leper. Gradually, I realized I had become one with the perverse disease. I had it in my heart.

But had I not spent the day holding a thousand hearts as far as I could from my own, using all my clinical skill to see them as parts of human beings, as less than human beings, as fascinating specimens? Had I not committed the most despicable sin of a physician, silently reserving myself to myself and denying what compassion I might have by holding back from the proffered hand of a patient in need? Had I not told myself, the whole day through, that when night fell I would leave the lepers' hell, as when a medical student, I had left the body on the anatomy table, left the slide of syphilitic tissue beneath the microscope, had left the caged rats in the physiology laboratory, left them to enjoy myself in the living world? Had I not contracted leprosy in the very act of fending it off? My heart felt weak.

What to do? I had asked Dr. Pandya if there was anything I could do. She had hesitated a moment, as though a bit embarrassed and said, ''I know you are from the States and you said your wife is meeting you by way of Hawaii. Should she go to Molokai, I would appreciate a picture of Father Damien's grave. I know they dug up his body and shipped it back to Europe, but I believe his heart is still there. If you could get me a snapshot of his grave—it doesn't have to be in color—it would help.''

And there it was—I could do something, but I could do nothing. I could do nothing directly to relieve the lepers of Bombay, but I could recognize that there are some who do help. There are some very few, who touch the spirit of mankind as deeply as leprosy repels it. Perhaps there is a cure for leprosy, but it will only come from those few who have the heart to be greater than the disease.

As though released by that flash of belief, a great sob welled from within me, and almost as though I could wash my spirit as I had washed my body, I found myself crying. I cried, and cried, and cried, and cried. Leprosy is truly a disease of the heart.

The Secret Service
of the Little Sisters

Leading everyday lives in small groups, they are one of
the most active Religious Orders in the world

By JAMES H. WINCHESTER

Five women share an apartment in a tenement in Chicago's inner
city. They earn their living packing boxes in a discount store, frying
hamburgers at a fast-food outlet, helping care for the elderly and mentally handicapped in a nursing home, and cleaning up in a school caf-
eteria.

- Three women in California live in a trailer, traveling with a tent
  circus, sewing costumes, selling soft drinks in concessions, and
  fashioning sequined blankets for the elephants and other parade
  animals.
- Far up on Little Diomede Island, in the middle of the Bering Strait
  which separates Alaska from Siberia, two women, one French and
  the other Swiss, share the harsh life of the local Eskimos. They
  melt ice for water, treat and cut furs, sew skins for clothes.

Together with 1,300 others of fifty-nine different nationalities, all
of these women are members of the Little Sisters of Jesus. With headquarters in Rome, this Order now has 215 Communities in over sixty
countries. All are guided by the inspiration of Little Sister Magdeleine,
who founded the group forty-one years ago in the Sahara Desert in
Algeria:

"You should look on the map of the world and see if there is not
a handful of men who, precisely because they are only a handful, are
of interest to no one. You should choose to go there, because otherwise

no one else may ever go to tell them that Jesus loves them and that He died for them.''

In small groups of usually three or four, the Little Sisters of Jesus work outside the usual Religious channels, living among the poorest and most unfortunate as members of their communities. Their model is the love Jesus showed as He lived so long and so unacknowledged among the common people of Nazareth.

As a Little Sister in Chicago said, ''We try to bring love and respect to the poor just as Jesus did. We want our home to be like Nazareth for others, a place of joy and peace and love. We share with our neighbors the dangers, such as fires, and the inconveniences like mice and rats and garbage in the alley. Still, we don't give half of what we receive from the people all around us.''

Little Sister Michelle is the coordinator for all Little Sisters of Jesus Fraternities, as they are called, in the U.S. and the Caribbean. She recently spent a week with Little Sisters traveling with the Vargas Circus in California.

''It is hard for the circus people to belong to a parish,'' she says. ''They work on Sundays. They are moving all the time. There really are no days off for them.

''We are the Church that goes with them. We learn from them how to live; to bear witness that God loves you already the way you are. There's a chapel in our truck, and show people can stop in there to pray. I know I would certainly want to go and pray someplace if I were going up on a high wire with no net below. But with this circus in America we are relatively new. Right now, we are getting to know the people and they are getting to know us.''

Circus owner Cliff Vargas is happy to have the Little Sisters around his tents. ''It's a good feeling. The nuns provide a sense of protection.''

A Little Sister in Montreal takes time to reflect on her duties: ''I've been working in the garment industry for six years. Sometimes, when I'm tired out from the noise and the monotony of the work, I ask myself, 'Why did I choose this? What good is it? Isn't there a better way to be at the service of the Church?'

''My heart quickly finds an answer. It's the concrete way in which I live the ordinary, hidden life of Nazareth at the heart of a big city, and above all at the heart of the world of 'little people,' those who have to work hard to earn their daily bread. It's the way I can be a 'savior with Jesus' in the sharing of their lives.

"Everybody knows that I'm consecrated to God and that I belong to the Church, even if some only have a vague idea of what that means. So I have to act accordingly; I'm a witness to Jesus, and people are watching me live. The world of working people is easy to love, but it often sees the Church as far away, mysterious, or simply unknown.

"My factory is a United Nations in miniature, with all its problems. My co-workers come from the West Indies, Brazil, China, Greece, Italy, Portugal, Morocco, and Colombia. Canadians are usually in the minority. Trying to get to know each person, and to love them with the heart of God, isn't so easy. Nor is it easy to be an element of unity when there is a disagreement, or during a little going-away party, or when a new immigrant worker arrives and everybody is looking at her out of the corner of an eye.

"But respectful and freely offered friendship is precious. There can be a thousand ways to express it: at the time of a death, an illness, an anniversary, or when somebody gets her citizenship. There are also the small ways of lending a hand: finding the information that newly arrived immigrants don't know where to get; helping a former co-worker get a job in a new factory; explaining the medical benefits under a union contract.

"Twice I've had to change factories because I wasn't working fast enough for the salary we were getting. But that's what sharing insecurity means; many others have to go through the same thing.

"Looking back—five factories in four years, all those faces I've seen and have come to know and love—it seems that Jesus has been asking me to bring a note of unity to my working milieu; unity among classes, nations, and races. Compassion, too, for often there is nothing to do but love and suffer together. As a Sister of Jesus, if I can only be a small sign of God's tenderness, it's worth it all.''

On the outskirts of Casablanca, Morocco, Little Sisters have lived for the past twenty-five years in a shantytown leper colony. Others live with Lapps and their wandering reindeer in Norway and Finland. In a small fishing village in Martinique, two Little Sisters of Jesus spend their days remaking mattresses for local residents. Still others are in Rwanda, the Cameroons, and Uganda in Africa, or in Afghanistan, Vietnam, or New Guinea.

In San Clemente, 9,000 feet high in Mexico's mountains, Little Sisters of Jesus live with the Otomi Indians, the poorest in a nation of the poor. Home for the Sisters is a hut with leaves for a roof and dirt for a floor. They sleep on the ground, lucky to have a blanket to wrap themselves in against the bitter night cold of the high altitude. Crops from rocky fields on steep slopes are poor at best.

The Little Sisters, like the Otomi with whom they share their lives, work hard. Grinding corn by hand to make tortillas is no easy task. They tend fires and help take care of the children. They are goat-herders. Sitting on rocks, they spin the fiber from local manguey plants into thread, which is later worked into a netlike material with many uses: head-coverings, back packs for children, and sacks to carry either wood from the mountains or produce to valley markets.

One of the San Clemente Little Sisters said, "To share with our Otomi brothers a life so hard, the way Jesus shared our human lot, is a constant call to faith. It is an adventure of discovery for us and our neighbors. In the simplicity and wealth of their hearts, and because of their material poverty, they live intensely the attitudes of dependence on God, of sharing, detachment; patience, gentleness, the rejoicing in simple things. This down-to-earth Gospel is the treasure they share with us."

The Little Sisters embrace the poor of all faiths. In Asia and the Middle East, for example, they live and work with Eastern Rite Catholics like the Coptic, Ethiopian, Syro-Malankar, Chaldean, Syrian, Melkite, Armenian, and Maronite. One-quarter of all the Little Sisters are good neighbors in Muslim countries. The Sisters' precept is: "Love without exception all men as brothers of Jesus and as your brothers. Live together with all races, nations, and backgrounds as a sign of universal brotherhood. Following the example of Jesus, the universal Savior, who loved all men infinitely and without exception, no single social group, race, people, or any man whatever will be barred from your love."

Much of the philosophy of the Little Sisters of Jesus comes from French priest Charles de Foucauld. A well-to-do son of an aristocratic Strasbourg family, he didn't enter the priesthood until he was forty-three. Charles wanted to live much as Jesus had lived in Nazareth before his public ministry. Not finding what he sought in the Trappists, he dreamed of establishing a new Religious Order and turned to the Sahara, where there were no priests.

His aims were simple. He would have only a lowly hermitage where a few monks could live on barley harvested by their own hands. This little Community would practice universal charity, sharing the little they had with whoever should come, guest or stranger. They would receive every human who knocked at their door, whether traveler or soldier, Christian, Muslim, Jew, or pagan.

In the fall of 1901, he established his first doors-always-open center in the Sahara Desert. He attracted tribesmen and travelers, but he was never able to attract other priests to share his way of life. One young Brother did join him for a few months in 1906, but left when the conditions seemed too hard.

Eventually, Foucauld established a center at Tamanrasset in the Algerian Sahara, among the Tuareg tribesmen. In December, 1916, he was alone when a raiding desert tribe broke down his door, entered, and murdered him.

Though Charles died thinking himself a failure, his dream did not die. In 1933, Father Villaume and four other young men in France left for Algeria, determined to follow in his footsteps, implementing the rule he had left for the proposed new Order of Little Brothers of Jesus.

These five established a monastery south of Oran at El Abiodh Sidi Chek. By 1936 there were ten Brothers at the isolated oasis. As more men were attracted to the new Order, the small Fraternities began to disperse to other parts of the world: Marseilles and the industrial north in France; the mining district of Belgium; Hamburg in Germany; Málaga in Spain. By the end of the 1950's, the Little Brothers of Jesus were established in the Middle and Far East, throughout Africa and in South and North America. Today 270 Brothers work in forty different countries.

"Where I sow, others will reap," Brother Charles had prophesied. Now five Religious Congregations, three of women, and two of men, carry on his work.

The Little Brothers and Little Sisters of the Gospel were founded by Father Villaume to begin active evangelization of the people among whom they live. They both have Fraternities on New York's Lower East Side.

The Little Sisters of Jesus were founded in 1939 at Touggourt in the Sahara in Algeria by a French nun, Sister Magdeleine. They were made a Diocesan Congregation in Aix-en-Provence in 1947, and established as a Pontifical Congregation by the Holy See in 1964. Little Sister Magdeleine, now well over eighty, still remains active in the Order.

The United States headquarters is in Washington, D.C., in a 100-year-old former farmhouse at Irving and 7th Street NE, in the middle of a blue-collar residential district. This is where women come to stay while deciding whether they want to join the Society. Sister Michelle and eight other Little Sisters live and work there. For money, they make religious articles to sell in the neighborhood.

The minimum age for joining the Little Sisters of Jesus is eighteen, but most candidates are several years older when they enter. One, Little Sister Mariette, is a widow with four grandchildren.

Initial training takes two years, one at a Formation Fraternity, the other living and working at some Fraternity somewhere else, maybe in a Hong Kong harbor junk or in the slums of a South American city.

During their training all Little Sisters try to master French and English. After they take their vows, the Little Sisters can be assigned anywhere in the world. Of the twenty-six Little Sisters assigned to the U.S.–Caribbean region only eleven grew up in the area. In India, the Little Sisters wear a blue sari, and in other countries where there is a national dress for women, their habit is adapted to it. In most of the world their usual habit is a blue working dress with a brown leather belt. For a veil, they wear a blue head scarf.

All Little Sisters take vows of poverty, chastity, and obedience. They also declare they will take on no formal Church duties, nor will they teach or work as supervisors of anything. One Little Sister out of ten can take a job as a nurse or a laboratory assistant, or work in an office, but never as a boss of any sort.

The Little Sisters of Jesus must have the local bishop's permission to establish themselves in any diocese, but they receive no financial or other material support. The money they earn from their jobs, less a small percentage to support regional and world headquarters, is what they must live on.

Each Fraternity has one room set aside as a chapel, where Little Sisters, and any neighbor, can pray and meditate. But the real business of the Little Sisters is in the day-to-day, real-life imitation of the hidden life of Jesus in Nazareth.

IV

COURAGE
TO LOVE WITH
GOD'S LOVE:
LOVE HEALS
PEOPLE

The Doll That Spoke

*The deaf mute prayed for a way to restore speech to a
badly frightened little girl*

By L. J. MEDUNA, M.D., with IRWIN ROSS

A nyone seeing Frank in my consultation room could have seen that
he had had more than his share of suffering. His face was marred
by a broken nose; it gave him a comic, grotesque look, like a sad clown.
But he carried a far worse burden: he was deaf and mute.

And so I expected to find a dull resignation in his eyes. I couldn't
have been more wrong. Frank's blue eyes were glowing and young and
cheerful.

And there was another surprise. Frank had broken his nose in a fall
some ten years before. And yet, although it interfered seriously with
his breathing, he had waited all those years before coming to a doctor
to have it fixed. Why? Frank told the story.

Frank hadn't been born a deaf mute. Up to the age of four he had been
a perfectly normal youngster. Then one evening as he was being tucked
into bed he complained, "Mama, my throat hurts. Bring me a glass of
water, please?"

The next day Frank was somewhat listless and complained again
about his throat. His mother decided that it was a cold coming on and
kept him in the house all day. The following day was the same, and
the next day, too. Finally, disdaining further concealment, the enemy
showed itself for what it was. When the family doctor arrived, the
situation was grim.

Diphtheria will declare itself in one of two ways: either dramatically,
with high temperatures and severe headaches, or, as in Frank's case,
with a slow, seemingly innocuous build-up. By the time Frank's disease

85

was diagnosed, most of the damage had been done. That he pulled through at all was due only to his sturdy constitution and his mother's devoted care. But the disease had destroyed his hearing and scarred his throat so badly that he could not speak.

At first Frank was puzzled. But his blue eyes slowly became bitter as he understood the terrible thing that had happened to him. He would wake up morning after morning thinking that now, in the light of day, the bad dream would be over.

His family lavished attention on him, but Frank's sense of betrayal only increased. At the school for the deaf, where he was sent, he could never get himself to join in with the others. The one question blotted out everything else: Why? Why did this have to happen?

Frank tried his hand at half a dozen trades but couldn't last in any of them for more than a week. He was always aware of the inquisitive, pitying glances of those around him; and added to his bitterness was a growing sense of self-pity.

Then Frank picked out a job for himself. At the time it gave him a certain perverse pleasure. Surely this was the right place for him—in a world of little creatures as silent and unhearing as he. The job was in a doll factory.

With his long, agile fingers, Frank soon became adept at putting the final delicate touches to each day's quota of rosy-faced dolls, and he was regarded as one of the company's most valuable employees. But he remained as solitary as ever.

When Frank slipped on the stairs one day and broke his nose he was almost glad. Here was another reason to feel sorry for himself. He would not think of having the nose repaired. It gave him pleasure to suffer.

Then one spring evening Frank, now in his twenties, noticed a change in his neighborhood.

Down the block lived the Caulder family; husband, wife, and five-year-old daughter Carol. Carol, a freckled, charming child, was always racing up and down the block on her scooter. She had tried often to talk to Frank as he trudged home in the evenings but, of course, had gotten no reply. After she found out that he could never talk, she would gaze at him with silent pity.

This Tuesday evening Frank noticed that Carol wasn't playing on the sidewalk as usual. Getting home, he asked his sister in a written note: ''What's happened to Carol Caulder?'' His sister pronounced the answer slowly and Frank read her lips.

''Diphtheria.''

But Carol's case was different from Frank's. Hers had the violent onset, aching throat, and high temperature, and the doctor was in no doubt as to the identity of the disease. He administered some medication at once, and the deadly, grayish green web that had begun to form over throat and tonsils was magically cleared.

But, though Frank's and Carol's cases were so dissimilar, Carol too seemed to have turned into a deaf mute.

The doctor assured her distraught parents that this could only be temporary. The throat had not been scarred and the hearing mechanism was intact. But silent day followed silent day. She simply would not speak.

The doctor confessed that he was stumped. But, learning all this, Frank wasn't stumped. He knew exactly what Carol felt: that her parents had somehow betrayed her. The disease had attacked with all its savagery right from the beginning. To Carol it seemed that her parents had suddenly changed from loving, all-powerful people into two strangers who just let you suffer.

Her answer, one might say her revenge, was to turn her back on this puzzling, cruel world; to retreat into silence.

Never before had Frank been concerned about another human being. He had always been too busy feeling sorry for himself. But he *knew* what was going on in Carol's mind and he wished to help her. That evening, for the first time in his life, he prayed. He asked that he be shown how to persuade Carol to speak.

That night Frank had a dream: he saw himself at his bench in the doll factory, and he was working on the most beautiful doll he had ever seen. Somehow he knew that it was to be for Carol.

The next day Frank received permission from his employer to make a very special doll for the sick girl. Never before had he taken such care with a doll. It was a beauty.

When he finished the doll, Frank inspected it, and thought: Please make Carol talk! Just a few words, just two or three words, but please, *make her talk!*

After work that afternoon he tucked the doll in a bright red-ribboned package and went to the Caulder's apartment. When Mrs. Caulder came to the door he gave her the package. A note was attached to the ribbon. "For Carol," it said.

Frank saw her smile and read the words of thanks on her lips and somehow felt better than he ever had since he could remember.

But that night, he became doubtful again. Carol had been given all sorts of presents during her sickness. She had turned away from all of them. How could his doll be any different? Yet the dream had been so clear!

In the middle of the night the telephone rang in Frank's apartment. Frank's sister answered it. The voice on the wire was so excited that for a minute or two Frank's sister did not recognize it as Mrs. Caulder's.

Mrs. Caulder seemed to be laughing and crying at the same time. She had an extraordinary story to tell.

That afternoon she had given Carol Frank's doll and explained from whom the present had come. Carol had looked at the doll dully and pushed it off her bed to the floor. Close to despair, the parents had sat silently through dinner and gone to bed early.

A few hours later Mrs. Caulder had felt a small hand on her arm. Startled, she had turned on the bedside light. Carol stood there. For the first time in weeks the mother heard her daughter's voice again.

"Mama," Carol said, "may I have a glass of water?"

"Darling!" Mrs. Caulder cried. "Of course you may! Anything you want!"

"It's not for me," Carol explained. "It's for the doll Mr. Frank brought me. She woke me up just now to tell me. I guess she must be feeling sick like I did a while ago. She said her throat hurt. She asked me to get her a glass of water."

You may or may not accept Carol's assurance that the doll actually talked. But when I saw Frank's bright, cheerful eyes in my office that day, I knew beyond all doubt that his prayer had been answered.

How Tina
Learned
She Was
Loved

*An odd, special incident helped me finally get through to
our adopted daughter*

By A MOTHER

How does it feel to be eight years old and not wanted by your parents? Most of us will never know. But Tina knows.

The day the caseworker brought Tina for a visit, my husband and I were nervous. But when I saw the anxiety in her big blue eyes, my nervousness gave way to sympathy. How does it feel to be a child who has to talk with strangers to find a suitable home?

We sat like statues in our living room while her eyes wandered to our two dogs, the trees outside the window, and the ceiling that needed painting. When asked if she had any questions, she looked me straight in the eye. "Do you have any other boy friends?" Now there's a question I don't hear every day. When I assured her that I was happy with just Jim, she turned to him.

"Do you get drunk very much?" How does it feel to be a child and see strange men brought home by your mother and eventually see your father, raving drunk, shoot one of them before your eyes?

Luckily for us, we met with Tina's approval, and she moved in on an unforgettable Friday. Our daughter Beth was home from college for the occasion and was looking forward to meeting her little sister. Would three o'clock ever come? I dusted things that didn't need dusting, Jim fixed things that didn't need fixing, and Beth almost brushed the dogs bald.

At last the car pulled into the driveway. We dashed out, the dogs at our heels. Tina climbed out of the car, gingerly carrying all her worldly possessions in a cardboard box. Both dogs gleefully jumped all over her, and made her drop her package. All of us began to pick up the scattered clothing. Then I looked at Tina. She had both thin arms across her face, and was sobbing softly and whimpering. "I didn't mean to drop it. Please don't hit me."

My heart sank. I'd never seen real fear and utter misery in a child's eyes before.

"Of course you didn't, honey," Beth said, and tried to put her arms around her. Tina pulled away, picked up the filled box, and headed toward the house.

Realizing how sad her life had been, we went all out to make her like us and our home. I cooked her favorite foods, and Jim catered to her every whim. In trying to build up her confidence, we inadvertently let her get by with childish pranks we'd never tolerated from Beth at her age.

Most of the time Tina was polite, sometimes overly so. Evidently, she did like us and didn't want to take any chances of our shipping her out. If your own mother deserts you, what can you expect from strangers?

One day she asked, "If I get really sick in the middle of the night, what can I do?" When assured she could call on me, she looked skeptical. "Don't you and Daddy Jim go out after I go to sleep?" How does it feel to be younger than eight, wake up sick, and find you're on your own?

The first few months with Tina were filled with many trials and mixed emotions. She was well behaved on the whole, but she didn't show us any affection and was leery if we got too close to her. She seemed almost to worship the dogs, though, and had long conversations with them. I even broke down and let Trixie, the little poodle, sleep at the foot of Tina's bed. Usually, she was in Tina's arms by morning.

The episode that changed our relationship with Tina was a special, odd kind of miracle. One Saturday afternoon, when I went out for the newspaper, I heard car brakes screech and a man yell. I looked up in time to see Tina swerve on her bike, laugh at the driver, and dare him to hit her. I saw red.

I grabbed a good, keen branch from the closest tree and marched Tina into the house, switching her legs as we went. I ordered her to bed.

She cried. Great, heaving sobs in total abandonment. This was the first time I'd ever known her really to cry, as a child cries. Once she'd caught her fingers in the car door and didn't utter a sound; she just pulled her lips tightly together and wrung her hands. It was so unnatural, it gave me an eerie feeling. (Later I learned that Tina had been beaten for crying.)

I made her supper as I cursed myself for being so cross with her and actually switching her legs. After all, this child had been through hell and wasn't responsible for the outlandish ways she had of demanding attention. I was full of pity for her and disgust with myself.

The supper tray held all her favorites: hot dog, potato chips, cookies, and a big milkshake. I'd apologize and try to make right what I'd done.

Tina looked up at me with red, swollen eyes. "Will you stay with me while I eat?" For once in my life I had sense enough to keep my mouth shut and only say, "Yes, I'll get myself a cup of coffee."

After eating like a football player, she peered at me apprehensively and said, "I think I deserved that spanking. But I didn't think you'd really do it!"

Apology forgotten, I took my cue. "Well, I did, honey. And I will again, anytime it's necessary. Jim and I love you, and it would break our hearts if you were badly hurt."

She stared at me unbelievingly, but wanting so hard to believe. I added, "And that's not the whole point. The poor man driving that car was scared out of his wits. He didn't want to hit you. His feelings count, too. You and I are not the only ones with feelings."

"Bozo and Trixie have feelings, too," she said. Then she actually grinned! "I love you and Beth and Daddy Jim, too," she said.

"And we love you," I replied, feeling as though I'd burst.

Tina is twelve now. She's never been physically punished since that day when she was eight. She has been sent to her room, curtailed in her activities, and talked to—sometimes quite loudly. She's a typical twelve-year-old; sweet, unpredictable, idealistic, and knows far more than any of the elderly set, which is anyone over eighteen!

How does it feel to be twelve years old and know you're loved and essential to a close family circle? Now Tina knows.

When
Leroy Came
to
Our House

*The five-year-old fought, threw rocks, stole, and used
language that would shame a platoon sergeant*

By S. HARRIS, as told to IRWIN ROSS

Nearly all the thirty-two children gathered at the country railroad
station were under control. A few were shouting and giggling.
Most stood and shuffled in patient embarrassment. Only one little fellow
was in open rebellion. Darting in and out and around, yelling obscen-
ities, hurling gravel at the parked cars, he was putting on a one-man
show of remarkable proportions for his size.

"That little roughneck," a man behind me said. "He can't be more
than four or five." A striped jersey three sizes too big for him hung
off his knobby shoulders. His trousers had been stitched in a grotesquely
amateurish job. His sneakers, bright and new, served to point up the
age and filth of the rest of his clothing. Only by brute strength did one
of the chaperons manage to drag him to the group and hold him there
so that the process of assigning the children to their adult "hosts" could
begin.

These were children from the inner city areas of Chicago, invited to
spend two weeks in the country with families who volunteered as hosts in
a plan sponsored by several churches. My husband Bill and I were in that
group, waiting with the others for our guests to be introduced.

Assignments were started. The name of a child was called and the child stepped forward. Then a name from the adult group was called and, in most cases, a man and woman stepped forward to claim the child. The fourth name called was that of the little tough guy. He pulled away from the group with a swagger and stood in front sullenly.

Then, into the suddenly apprehensive stillness, fell my husband's name. We gave each other a look and, as we stepped out of the group, a general murmur of sympathy arose. Bill and I went forward to meet a boy named Leroy.

The ride home did nothing to relieve our rapidly growing fear. Leroy sat in the back and pulled my hair, kicked at the seat, yelled out the window, and doggedly ignored all attempts to interest him in the landscape or to lure him into conversation. His vocabulary would have shamed a platoon sergeant.

Finally at home, I tackled the problem of cleaning up Leroy and trying to get him settled for the night. While I was sorting his meager wardrobe, Leroy approached me like a truck, almost knocking me over, and informed me that he wanted to go home, that he didn't like me or anybody or anything here. To prove it he dumped a vase of flowers on the living room table.

Using the only method I could, plain strength, I dragged him to the bathtub for a struggle which did nothing to his personality but accomplished a near miracle in physical transformation. Suddenly he was a very small and quite handsome dark-eyed little boy. Defenseless he was not. He continued to be fresh, and aggressively disinterested during supper, which he ate ravenously. Afterward he demanded to be shown his bed, announcing again that he didn't like it here and was going home right after he slept.

Frightened and exhausted, I put him to bed, cleaned up the deluge he had created in the bathroom, put his clothes to soak and joined Bill in the living room where we sat staring at each other in mutual horror.

"Well," Bill said finally, "we didn't do it for *us*."

I put my hand in his in gratitude for the helpful reminder, and we sat there for a while remembering why we *had* done it.

* * *

It had started on the previous Christmas Eve. After a long day of wrapping and delivering gifts, Bill and I filled our baby Peter's sock and sat down to survey the lavish display that covered the better half of the room.

"One small two-year-old boy," Bill said, shaking his head. "And just look at all this. There's something immoral about it. Think of all the little children who don't have anything, kids who *know* it's Christmas. We don't do enough."

I'd often felt it. We gave to the Community Fund, a few national charities, and to our church. But we seldom *did* anything, seldom gave anything of ourselves.

I told Bill about a neighbor I'd once known. Every summer she had taken a child from the city slums for a two-week vacation here in the country.

"How about it?" Bill said, eagerly. "Let's give some little kid a ball next summer. Let's give someone a little bit of what we've got to give. A good home in a good town. Time, fun, good food."

I was gnawed by doubts. I considered the grim possibilities: getting a child who might in some way hurt our own Peter; being unable to help a homesick little stranger; having a child in our home who resented us for the presumption that we had more to give him than his own parents; giving a child a taste of comparative luxury, then sending him back to a world of poverty.

"Well, let's find out about it," Bill countered.

We did. We learned that, through various churches, each summer hundreds of underprivileged city children escape their hot and overcrowded homes. All transportation, liability insurance, and medical costs are met by the churches. Volunteer families like us supply the hospitality.

Now, some months after that Christmas Eve, a little boy named Leroy was sleeping in our guest room, and I was exhausted and troubled, worried about how I was to manage the next two weeks. But Bill was right. We hadn't done it for us. I went to check little Peter and then in to Leroy. To my shame I found that he had apparently been sobbing quietly ever since I had said good night. I went over and sat next to him on the bed.

"It'll be all right, Leroy," I told him. "We'll have lots of fun."

"No," he sobbed. "I want to go home to my own mama."

"But your mama wants you to stay and go swimming and ride horses for a few days before you go home."

"I don't want no horse ridin'," he cried. This was not the aggressive, wise, wound-up little roughneck of the railroad station, but a homesick, lonesome, very small child, barely five. Almost a baby. I tried to comfort him the way a baby needs to be comforted, with a kiss and a hug, stroking his head and shoulders until he fell asleep. It didn't take long, but it was long enough so that my own strength was renewed by the knowledge of his helplessness, his dependence on us. I knew simply that we must do the best we could for him.

For those first few days it wasn't easy. Leroy distinguished himself in the town by fist fights, stone throwing, and a snarling attitude toward the children. He pulled the buds and blossoms from the flower gardens. He turned the garden hose on hanging laundry. He dumped the trash barrel and pulled down the rose trellis.

He even stole. Once, he darted through the gang crowded around an ice cream vendor, clicked a handful of change out of the man's change clip, and scooted back out of the crowd again. For a moment even the chattering children were shocked into a stunned silence.

Shocked, too, I had to remind myself to keep calm and handled this firmly, unhysterically. I sent Leroy into the house, and returned the money to the ice cream man.

"Quick, isn't he?" I commented lightly.

"Fastest thing I ever saw," the man answered with a touch of both humor and admiration.

Instead of focusing on his small crime we had stressed Leroy's speed, and that was what remained in the children's minds.

There was the time he escaped me in the grocery store and returned laden with a whole ham, a chicken, and a package of chops.

"Send these to my mama," he ordered peremptorily. "Right away. She wants 'em right away." Could you scold a child for such a thing? I couldn't.

His fierce and affectionate loyalty to his family was always heartwarming.

"When my daddy gets a whole lotta money he's gonna buy me one of these" was a statement we heard several times daily. It might refer to a toy or to a horse, or even a car. More often than not his "Man, that's nuthin'!'' was accompanied by a brightening of his eyes, and we learned to recognize that Leroy was enjoying himself somewhere underneath his preoccupation with money.

Leroy was always gentle and affectionate toward Peter, although he was ever watchful that we weren't giving Peter more than him. I was reading *Peter Rabbit* to the boys when I suddenly noticed that tears were rolling down Leroy's cheeks.

"What's the matter, Leroy?"

Through his sobs he managed to explain that he was unhappy because I kept saying "Peter Rabbit" and hadn't once said "Leroy Rabbit." From then on every story I read to him was sure to have one major character named Leroy.

The poverty which Leroy knew in his own home was evident and heartbreaking. I remember his surprise at being given a toothbrush "just for myself!" His wonder at the big bed in which he slept "without my brothers!" I think of his horror when other children idly fed ends of hot dogs or ice cream cones to their dogs.

Always, always, even at his best, money was foremost in Leroy's mind. On his last night, we had arranged a farewell cookout for him. When the guests had all left I went into the house to find Leroy sitting pensively in the middle of the living room floor. He looked up as I came in.

"Man, that sure was somethin' you done for me," he said. "Musta cost a whole lotta money. I'm gonna get some money and buy one for you and one for my mama and daddy." And he responded warmly to my affectionate hug.

I haven't any indication that Leroy changed while he was with us, only that at last he allowed us to see some of his natural childlike sweetness. And we learned not to expect or want change in him, but to love him just as he was.

Leroy was, I think, not only for us but for others in our town a warming experience. Friends and neighbors contributed so much good clothing, both new and used, that we had to mail two large boxes to his home. The owner of the local children's clothing shop refused payment for the socks and underwear I selected for Leroy. When I took out a bill to pay the barber for Leroy's haircut, the barber waved it aside with, "First one's on me." When Leroy developed a small infection on his knee our family doctor treated it without charge. One ten-year-old boy devoted hours to teaching Leroy the arts of fishing, rowing, and swimming.

What we gave Leroy, if anything, we are not sure. Love we gave him, but he is secure in his own family's love. He had a good time, we know. He looks forward as we do to his coming back to us next summer.

V

COURAGE TO LOVE WITH GOD'S LOVE: LOVE DRAWS PEOPLE CLOSER TO GOD

One
Christmas
Eve

*A true story found among the effects of an American
soldier killed in action thirty-six years ago*

By JAMES WOLFGRAM

It began as a trickle: an occasional *papasan* with tall hat and crooked cane leading wailing women and children down the slippery mountain trails that led to the beach at Wonsan, North Korea.

Behind them sounded the dull thunder of artillery. With each muffled burst came a bitter memory of their ruined villages, whose younger men had been systematically slaughtered by the Chinese Communist army advancing south from Chosin Reservoir. Before them lay a vast fleet waiting to pick up retreating U.S. Marine and Army units.

Soon the trickle became a flood, a stream of humanity that poured from the mountains six days and nights, intermingled at times with gaunt, bearded Americans, heads down and faces immobile.

Little by little the boats were loaded. The 100,000 weak refugees begged to be put aboard. They had been subsisting on C-rations and whatever else they could forage.

Amid the embarkation came four American soldiers of the 10th Engineer Battalion of the 3rd Infantry Division. They had been fighting a rear-guard action for a Marine regiment that had arrived on the beach the previous day. One, a corporal named King, told the beach commander that the rest of his unit had been captured or killed. The four men boarded a ship already filled with civilians.

His men secured, King set out to find a medic to treat his frostbitten fingers. He stumbled through the crowd of huddled refugees and suddenly tripped. To a cacophony of Korean chatter, he screamed an obscenity. The past month of combat, carnage, and misery swiftly combined with the pain in his fingers, and his feeling of futility was finally unleashed. He fell.

A wrinkled hand touched his face and he looked up to see a yellowtoothed grin. An old man was saying something to him, but King's gaze was fixed on the beard, about ten long strands that flowed from his chin, the mark of a village elder. The old man took King's good hand in his and in sign language asked if he could borrow the mitten to cover the feet of a shivering child nearby. Why not? King thought.

A South Korean soldier came up to them and, in his best pidjin English, told King that the old man was grateful and would like to offer something in return for the mittens. The elder, he said, had heard King yell the word *God* before he fell to the floor and that was why he felt bold enough to ask for the mitten, for the old man was a Christian, too. He had not understood the rest of King's curse.

The old man removed his back sack, and King wondered how anyone so skinny could be so agile. He used only one flowing motion of his left hand; the right remained tucked in his shirt. He rummaged for a while and gently removed a small plaster statue of the Christ Child, Joseph, and Mary.

"He wants you to have it," the Korean soldier said. "A missionary gave it to him many years ago. He says that now he is like Christ's father and he welcomes the pain."

King studied the man as he slowly pulled his right arm from his shirt. There was only a bloody cloth-covered stump. "The Communists cut the hand off when they came to his village," the soldier said.

King looked at the statue. The right hand of Joseph had been chipped off, too.

"He wishes you a most joyous Christmas," the Korean soldier continued. "He wants to know whether it is today or tomorrow that is the traditional eve of Christ's birth."

"Today," King told the interpreter, just realizing that it was December 24, 1950.

When I Went Looking
for Room for Christ

*A Mexican Christmas, a friendly priest, and a dark-eyed
boy helped me leave grief behind*

By HELEN HAYES

W hen you have lost someone who is dearer to you than life itself,
the gaiety and heedlessness of a fiesta crowd is bewildering. You
wonder how anybody can possibly be so elated when it is plain to you
that this is a lonely world. When a close loved one died some years
ago, my son and I tried to weather a siege of loneliness and bittersweet
memories by going to Cuernavaca, Mexico. We arrived at the start of
the Christmas season.

But I was just not ready for the fiesta spirit that surged over the
walls and in through my open windows. I was an alien and I knew it,
an alien alone on an island of grief.

For a place of solace I found a beautiful old Franciscan church on
the cathedral square. I discovered I could pray in that church; and when
I could not pray, it was comfortable just to sit there, watching the
brilliant sunshine streaming through the old Spanish door and reflecting
on the griefs and joys that had come through it in two and a half
centuries.

After a few visits to the church, I began hearing a lot about one of
its young priests, Father Wasson, a man of very large heart. I made it
a point to see him for myself.

Father Wasson is large, shy, and guileless-looking. He is accom-
plishing a quiet revolution in Mexico. Well, not exactly quiet—boys
are not the stuff that quiet is made of, but quiet in the sense that there
is no fanfare. About fifteen years ago he started taking in boys who

had been in trouble with the law. Now he has cared for well over a thousand.

Exactly how he clothes and feeds all those children not even he is sure. Except that he has many friends—in Mexico, in the U.S., Canada, and in heaven. The friends, are, indeed, part of the miracle—they prove that goodness is contagious.

Once he had to borrow money from the sewing woman to buy tortillas for the week. Another time when there was absolutely nothing in the cupboard, he got a large check from a stranger. When he really needs something, when the need is tangible and desperate, he doesn't go to the local bank, he *prays* for what he needs. Somebody promptly comes along and gives him just enough money. To him this is an admirably simple system.

Just when you have decided that he is a nice uncomplicated soul, left over from the early Franciscans, you discover that he is also a college professor and a psychiatrist. I know these things now, but I didn't then. He struck me, as he does many people on first acquaintance, as someone who has wandered out of a storybook and should not be allowed to bruise himself on our sophisticated problems.

Father Wasson took me to see his children, and I saw them at their best, all scrubbed and shining for Christmas season. In Mexico, Christmastime is a totally religious holiday, with no gifts. It actually begins with an event called a posada on the evening of the sixteenth. In the Latin custom, this is Christ's birthday and He should get the gifts. This I found very beautiful.

My anguished heart was soothed by the look in the children's eyes; this world was still magic for them, cold or no cold, hunger or no hunger. When you see the great, solemn, shining eyes of the children, you reach out, you think, *Heaven is still there, if only I can touch it.* I reached out timidly, gropingly, and found a small warm hand that was little-boy grubby but magnificently understanding. And so I met Rudi.

Someday Rudi will break somebody's heart with those great limpid eyes. He was a little rascal whose time in the streets had not been wasted, and he had the face of a Murillo cherub.

Rudi escorted me through the posada. Each evening, just as the stars began to push through the curtain of a green and lavender sky, we all lined up and began the posada, a sort of pageant right out of the

Middle Ages where you go from door to door unsuccessfully seeking a lodging for Jose, a poor carpenter, and his wife Maria. Four little boys carry the litter with the statues of San Jose and his wife Maria. And down the centuries come the litany of excuses:

"I cannot let you in, Lord, because important people would be embarrassed by You."

"I cannot let You in because I am so busy grubbing for some wealth to leave behind me."

"I cannot let You in because You have no social standing."

"I am too busy. I am too busy. Go away."

"I cannot let You in because hate has sealed the door."

Rudi, as gallant as any knight of old Castile, escorted me from door to door, looking at my face from time to time to see how I was taking it. As we walked along, singing the endless verses of the old chant, I could not have stopped if I had wanted to. Neither of us knew the other's language, but I heard him loud and clear. The grand, sonorous prayers I had said as a child came back to me.

At the very summit of the Christmas season is the Day of the Kings, the day of gifts for the children. Rudi's uncontained excitement fizzed over into the silent gardens of my heart. Alerted by his great zest for living, I too began to scan the horizon for those three mysterious figures to come riding out of the East to bring gifts: Caspar on his fine Arabian horse, Melchior on a stately camel, and Balthasar the Ethiopian on a great gray elephant. All my life I had lived with the make-believe of the theater and a world shaped with the magic of words. Now, wordless, a fantastic little actor was weaving around me a world of make-believe that was part and parcel of this great fiesta of light. You had to be a child to fully comprehend, but with Rudi's help I did pretty well.

Every step I took in the posada was a going back; every drop of my Irish blood reminded me that I had once been a citizen of Rudi's world of unquestioning trust in an all-provident Father in heaven.

Over the next days I reflected that God had been very good to me through the years of an interesting life. God gave and He took away and I had not been as meek as Job about it. Finally I asked Father Wasson to instruct me for my return to the Church from which I had drifted years ago.

Like others of Father's earthly friends, I tried to help him get some money for the ever-growing needs of his family. We talked a beautiful station wagon out of the Rotary Club of Cleveland, Ohio. We sought by a dozen means to pull together the poles of supply and demand. Sometimes this was sad work and sometimes we got angry. But I remember those enterprises most for the lovely laughter. We laughed in a beautiful knowledge that He is already doing the completely impossible.

All that was some years ago. But still, going back to Cuernavaca now is like going home. The wriggling, bright-eyed boys who smiled at me that first Christmas are gone now—most of them are teaching, some are married. And though their places have been taken by others of Mexico's beautiful chldren, Rudi and his friends—including wonderful Father Wasson, who still labors on—are not forgotten. They never can be. For they brought me a special gift that Christmas—not in a sack, tucked in with toothbrushes and new clothes and sugar cane. My gift came as an oasis of peace in a time of sadness—a gift of new love given me at a time when I desperately needed to love.

There is the time in every life, I think, a time of the star, a moment very dark when one must look up and—if he is wise—follow the light as the Magi did, a light that leads to love and hope.

The Woman
Who Wouldn't Pray

Not for the one who needed her prayers the most

By CAROL V. AMEN

The chaplain had tried everything with the woman but prayer—her prayer. Oh, he had prayed, ever since the doctors admitted there was nothing they could do but keep her comfortable. But she was so bitter, so alone and aloof. And, despite drugs, her last days were bound to be difficult.

It was while praying for her and a long list of others that he got the idea. He wondered if there was a chance. It certainly couldn't hurt.

"Sara," he said tentatively, "I know you have a great deal on your mind, but I want to ask a favor. There's a family that needs extra support just now. Their four-year-old daughter is in a coma. She's in the last stages of leukemia. They need strength to get through this."

Sara seemed puzzled. "What has this got to do with me?"

"I need help. Sometimes it's just too much for me. I pray daily for the people of this hospital, but I could use another voice, another heart. I'm asking you to pray for the family of little Carrie, to ask God to put his loving arms around them."

"Chaplain, I don't mean to be rude, but it's been a long time since I prayed. With my diagnosis, if I had any inclination at all, it would be to pray for myself."

"You may certainly do that," he said. "But I'm asking you to pray for others." He took her hand. "Please, Sara, for me. I get so discouraged."

Before she pulled her hand away, she nodded briefly.

Two days later he came back. Little Carrie had slipped peacefully into the next world, and her parents were as honest in their grief and as strong as any he had ever seen in the loss of a child.

Now he wished to ask another favor, for a teenager on a voluntary drug withdrawal program. The boy said he wanted to stay clean, but he feared he'd lose his nerve when he got back with his friends on the outside. Would she pray for him?

"I'm rusty," Sara said angrily. "Never did have the knack. I hated resorting to prayer only when I was in trouble, and it never occurred to me otherwise. It all seems so hypocritical."

"That's the reason I want you to pray for others," the chaplain said. "Surely you don't think God would question your motives in praying for Carrie's family or this teenager?"

She sighed. "It does give me something to do. When I begin to need a pain killer, I make myself pray for fifteen minutes before putting on the call light. It's silly, though."

On Tuesday he asked her to keep praying for the teenager, and also to add a man who'd suffered a stroke. The chaplain described the old fellow's frustration as he struggled to speak to his son and daughter-in-law. Though his hearing was not impaired, his family shouted all their questions and encouragements. "They can't make out what he's trying to say," the chaplain said to Sara, "but instead of listening harder, they simply yell louder."

"How's the boy?" Sara moved carefully, onto her side. "The one fighting drugs? With all the drugs I'm taking for pain I can certainly identify with him."

"The doctors released him yesterday. I asked him to stop and see me when he comes in for his appointment with the psychologist. I told him there were at least two people here praying for him. Is the pain getting bad?"

She lifted an eyebrow. "I play a new game with myself now. As the shots get more frequent, I also increase the length of my prayers. When I can't stand it any longer, I give myself a reward. Morphine." She smiled. "A pay-off for praying."

The chaplain's heart leaped. Less than two weeks ago she had nothing to spare, no sympathy, no energy for anyone, not even herself. Now he shared the plights he'd just learned of: a middle-aged woman who needed a kidney transplant, and a young couple whose much wanted baby had been born with Down's syndrome.

* * *

The following week Sara's deterioration was obvious. She spoke hardly above a whisper, and the floor nurses said the end was near. The chaplain described successful laser treatment on the eyes of an artist with detached retinas.

The next day he told her about an older woman the doctors suspected of having bone cancer. Her condition turned out to be a fairly mild form of arthritis. The chaplain asked Sara to give thanks for these events and others taking place throughout the hospital and the city.

When the boy came to see the psychologist, the chaplain persuaded him to visit Sara. At her bedside he watched the streetwise youth grope for words. "I feel stronger now," the boy said, the wonder apparent in his voice. "It's gotta be coming from somewhere. I tried to kick it twice before, and it didn't work. I gotta believe you must have some influence, lady." He paused, struggling.

"The chaplain here, though, he told me you ain't doing so good on your own case. I'm not in the know on this, but I been trying. I been . . ." He paused again. "I been pr-pr-praying for you." There. He'd said it. His glance went ceilingward, then back down at the woman in the bed. "Hang in there, lady." He hurried from the room.

Sara motioned the chaplain to come closer. He pulled a chair over so that their eyes were level. He recognized their pain, and also their joy.

"I saw through your little scheme almost from the start," she whispered. "But I still have to thank you. You've turned my last days into . . . into rather an interesting adventure."

"Don't thank me," the chaplain said, his voice husky. "Let's both thank Him together." He took her dry hands in his and began firmly. "The Lord is my Shepherd, I shall not want . . ."

She joined him and they repeated the words slowly, softly, in unison. By the time they got to "surely goodness and mercy," he was saying the psalm alone. His silent thanks poured forth as he sat holding Sara's hands and watching her quiet, even breathing. For the first time in weeks, she slept without the help of drugs.

Jenny, Yvonne, and the Secret of Happiness

God helps those who help each other

By ANGELA M. SCHREIBER

I keep searching for real happiness. But when I find it, it lasts for such a little while. I thought resuming my career would give me the satisfaction I lacked. Buying something new used to give me a lift. I've got a busy social life. I'm married to a man I'm in love with and we have beautiful children. I'm beginning to think I'm neurotic."

The distraught young woman sat talking with me across the kitchen table. I felt more than a little helpless, but I put the coffee on and encouraged her to talk.

I asked her how she defined happiness. She thought for a moment and replied, "Happiness is having your life well-ordered and being with the people you really care about. Happiness is having the things you need without a lot of worry about how you're going to get them. And happiness is success with your work. I have all that. But I keep looking for something else—something I can't define."'

Then an expression of fear, or perhaps doubt, crossed her face, and she said softly, "Unless what I'm looking for is God."

She had answered her own question, but she was clearly afraid of her answer. "If God is the Jesus Christ I have heard about all my life, how could He accept me? I don't always live by his rules. I'm not sure I even want to."

"From what I know of you, Jenny, I don't see that you're so far away from living a Christian life," I answered.

"Oh yes I am. I don't put myself out for other people. For instance, if I were you, I wouldn't take the time to listen to this foolishness I'm spouting off.''

That conversation took place years ago. I thought I had reasonable answers for Jenny. But we sorted through many things over a period of several months and she was still dissatisfied.

She even started going to church for the first time in her adult life. But she came away unhappy because she thought she should have some kind of overpowering feeling.

Then something happened that ultimately affected both of us. I had a new baby. And suddenly, it seemed that I would never know joy again. My tiny little girl was born with Down's syndrome.

In the depths of my soul, I blamed God. I felt that He had failed me; and worse still, He had failed my child, who had never deserved to come into the world imperfect.

Our close friends knew there was a grave problem with the baby before I came home from the hospital with her. No one quite knew how to handle it, so they stayed away. Everyone except Jenny.

Jenny was waiting for our arrival. She had a meal prepared and a lovely gift for Yvonne. (It wasn't convenient for her; she had taken the day off from a busy job.)

During those first difficult weeks, she dropped by in the evenings and stood up under my tears and my moods. I didn't tell her that I thought God had abandoned my baby and me, but she sensed my feelings.

One day she said, ''You know, I'm praying for Yvonne and you, too.'' I wanted to thank her. But I could not. My answer was silence. ''I know God exists,'' she said. ''I still haven't found Him, but I don't feel as much emptiness as I once felt.''

As time passed, and Yvonne grew, the joy within her reached out to me. Life began to be beautiful again.

Yvonne is nine years old now. Jenny dropped in to visit us last week and Yvonne greeted her with a big hug and kiss and lively conversation.

Later, Jenny said, ''By now, I suppose you know I've finally filled that void in my life. Yvonne came into my life, too. When I knew you needed me, I tried to help because you had listened when I needed someone.

"I even thought God had let you down. And I was aware that you did, too, but I couldn't let you know I agreed with you. I had never given quite that much of myself to anyone before, and as time went on, my dissatisfaction with myself dwindled. As giving became easier, I began to know God. If I had not learned that, I never would have found Him."

VI

COURAGE
IN PARENTHOOD:
TRUSTING GOD
WITH
YOUR CHILDREN

Diary of a
Reluctant Mother

*When I found out I was pregnant, I sat down on the
couch and started to cry*

By CAROL WEBER

He rests his little cheek against mine and takes in a sharp breath as
the spring breeze races across his neck. I whisper in his ear as I
walk, telling him about the flowers, the green oranges, and the breeze.

I'll tell my son many stories before he's grown. Someday I'll tell
him about being born. But I'll never tell him that he is the child I never
meant to have.

When I married John I was twenty-six. He was twenty-nine. Before
we were married we never discussed having children. We talked instead
of making money and traveling.

All too soon I was past thirty and we decided, definitely, that we
would never have children. Then, at thirty-five, I discovered I was
pregnant.

May 20, 1975: How do you tell your husband after nine years of
saying there will be no children that suddenly there is one?

I practiced: "We're going to be parents. We're going to have a
baby." Important to get the *we* in there, I decided.

When I got home, John was cooking dinner.

"I'm pregnant." I blurted it out as I walked in.

He turned around and shut the cabinet door. "That's just what I
needed," he said, and went back to stirring the stew.

I poured myself a glass of wine, sat down on the couch, and started
to cry. John came over and sat beside me. "Hey, what's wrong?"

"What's wrong? I'm pregnant, and I don't know what to do," I blubbered.

"What's to do? You're pregnant. So, you're going to have a baby. Drink the wine. Dinner's almost ready."

He leaned over and kissed my cheek.

June 6: Intimates call the doctor's office the baby factory. There are four doctors, so when your time comes you don't have to worry that the only soul who knows is on the golf course or in Europe.

The nurse takes down the basics. "Are you going to deliver the child?"

"What?" I have a sudden vision of trying to deliver my own baby.

She puts it in words I could understand: "Are you going to have the baby, or terminate the pregnancy?"

It's not every day you're asked a life or death question. This question is an offer of a way out. But I could not bear the guilt of not giving my child a chance to be born.

June 18: Whenever conversation turns to my having a baby, my palms sweat and my stomach churns. Thank God it takes nine months to make a baby. It will take me at least eight to get used to the idea.

July 1: Office visit. I watch one woman with a three-year-old boy at her knee. He is moving around too much to suit her. "Leave that magazine for one of the *good* children to read. If you don't behave, I'm going to take you in and have the doctor give you a shot." I know I can be a better mother than that. I feel better thinking about it.

July 6: What comes over people when they find out you're pregnant? People I barely know walk up and rub my arms, hug me, pat my belly. I think I'll scream.

July 10: End of three months. Feeling fine. I guess I should have known I was pregnant when I stopped liking beer. If I'm a connoisseur of anything, it's beer. But now I can't stand it.

August 1: A friend gave me a book called *Having a Baby* by Dr. Eric Trimmer. An English girl named Jane kept a diary from the day she suspected her pregnancy until delivery. Her doctor made marginal notes which explain what's happening medically as Jane describes it. The book is beautifully done, with pictures of Jane as her baby develops. It becomes my birth-bible. I find myself relating to Jane and enjoying my own pregnancy.

August 14: There are times when I have a flash of anxiety. I've been taken over by something I cannot control. Sometimes I feel I'm just a receptacle. That is *not* the way I want to feel.

August 20: Resting after getting John off to work. Dozing, one hand across my abdomen. Suddenly, a twitch—more than a twitch—a jerk like a muscle spasm. My eyes fly open. My heart starts to pound! It's alive! There's a living being in there. I don't want to go to work. I just want to lie here, experiencing. Quickening, it's called—as in the quick and the dead. Life.

August 26: "How's things?" Dr. K., smiling.

"Oh, swollen feet if I work too long. A little gas, some heartburn."

"Same old stuff, huh?" He pulls out a blue plastic device shaped something like an electric razor, with two sets of earphones. "Have you heard the baby's heartbeat?"

The nurse puts a greasy blob on my stomach and attaches the Doptone as I plug in the earphones.

Sloshing. Then "pocketa-pocketa-pocketa" very fast, six or eight beats.

Dr. K. picks up the Doptone and walks out. The nurse wipes off the grease blob and follows him. Swoosh, they are gone.

For a minute I think I had shouted at them to wait, to let me hear more, for hours maybe. But the voice was only in my mind. I blink back tears.

"Older parents tend to make better parents." Dr. K. is smiling at me. "How long have you been married?"

"Nine years."

"Had you tried to have children before and just not made it, or had you decided not to have any?"

"We decided we didn't care to have any."

"But you secretly did want one, obviously. Otherwise you would have had a legal abortion."

I am barely listening to him. I am hearing something else. "Pocketa-pocketa-pocketa-pocketa."

September 5: Sometimes, especially on Friday nights after a twelve-hour day, when I'm facing a long drive home from work, dinner to fix, and dishes to wash, I wonder how I'll ever cope with this and a child, too.

October 10: First real down spell. Cry over sad TV movie.

October 15: Mother writes she's dreaming it's a girl. Dentist looks at my gums and says it's a boy. ESP believer at work says it's a boy. Strange little man in drugstore tips his hat, says, "Excuse me, ma'am. It's going to be a girl. I know these things."

November 10: Two months to go. I thought I'd be used to the idea, but still wake up with a start sometimes thinking, "My God, I'm pregnant." As though I just learned it.

November 23: Put John on a plane to go hunting at my uncle's place in West Virginia. This is usually our annual trip together, but I'm concerned about being there such a short time before the baby's birth. After he's gone, I realize how very little John and I have talked about what's happening to us. Really talked.

Oh, sure, we talk about cleaning out the second bedroom and putting up wallpaper, but it hasn't been done yet. We tell each other we don't care whether it's a boy or a girl. I let him know I'm not afraid of childbirth but am not too sure about taking care of a baby after it's born. He insists he can show me all I need to know. He helped raise younger brothers and sisters. He's an expert.

December 20: John is funny and rather wonderful. His friends call him "father" and he grins foolishly. He still doesn't talk much about it. But John says all the things that are important, casually, as though he doesn't know how much it means to me to hear him tell a friend: "I'm not worried about her (having the baby). Carol does everything well. She'll do this well, too." And to me, 140 pounds, with swollen feet: "You're beautiful." And he insists I quit work now to wait.

Christmas: Our last Christmas alone. The tree is up. Many friends drop by. John buys enough Walt Disney wallpaper to start his own store and spends three days putting it up in the baby's room. (That still sounds funny—"baby's room.")

I can tell, it won't be much longer.

January 6: There's a great calm about me. I finish cleaning some cabinets; joke with a friend over dinner. Whenever I start to feel anxious, I get up and do more housework. Therapy is a good hot pan of dishwater.

11:00 P.M.: I know before we go to bed that this is it. I time my pains in the dark with John's new watch.

January 7, 3:00 A.M.: Sitting in a wheelchair in the emergency room. I'm not ready for this. Maybe it's false labor. Maybe they'll send me home.

Labor room: I'm alone in this place. My feet are cold. The warm socks the natural childbirth people remind you to take are in my suitcase, somewhere. It's a zoo here. Nurses and doctors laughing outside. I watch the clock, breathe deeply, count the seconds. At 6:45 A.M. I hear the nurse outside phoning my doctor. "Four centimeters, is still refusing medication." I feel noble. I also hurt.

A new nurse comes on duty. She will stay with me now until the end. Two more women are moved into the room. One is saying she wants medication at the first sign of pain. It's her second child. I'm losing control, now. Without someone to coach me through the breathing I'm getting tired, dozing in the minute and a half between contractions. It's been like this for more than two hours. I didn't expect the pains to be so close together so long.

7:15: I finally agree to a shot of Demerol. The doctor arrives and has an I.V. started. My water breaks. I hurt. If only my feet were warm!

The minutes pass and there are sounds from the delivery room next door: "Push."

"I can't take it any more."

"Of course you can. Push." A slap. A cry. It's a boy.

Three boys are born as I lie there. Mine must be a girl, I think.

Another contraction. I can no longer keep from moving against the pain. I have lost all self-consciousness. I can't wait for each examination so I can hear the progress report: five centimeters, six, seven.

"You can push now."

I am making terrible faces and straining noises. My breath is foul, my lips parched. I'm glad John is not here.

"Push. Don't waste that contraction."

I feel the baby drop into the birth canal. The curtains are swept aside, and I am whisked into the delivery room. I can see my doctor through the window, gowning up. He moves in slow motion. I want to yell for him to hurry up, but I concentrate instead on not pushing until he gets there.

I see no beauty in this. Awesome, fantastic, yes. But beautiful, it is not—not until it's over.

In the last seconds I remember a friend's advice. "Don't expect to feel overwhelmed with a sudden sense of motherhood when your baby is born. You might not feel that way until you really start caring for it." I have been clinging to that thought—in case.

I have been working hard. I am tired. I want it to be over with. The baby begins to emerge. The umbilical cord is wrapped around its neck. I am not afraid. I have read a lot. I know this is not unusual.

January 7, 9:50 A.M.: The baby is born. I forget to ask what it is, and the doctor turns him around. A beautiful, howling, bright-blue boy.

Minutes after he is born, the phone rings at the delivery room door. It's John. He's at the nearest bar, where the guys have a weight pool going. The baby is seven pounds, 11 ounces.

I laugh and joke with the doctor. The baby turns pink as he cries, pumping air into his lungs. I am proud of myself. I am mildly interested in watching the demise of the ice-blue umbilical cord, one of the most beautiful things I've ever seen, and the placenta, one of the ugliest.

"Do you want to hold him?"

Funny, I hadn't realized my hands had been tied down. The nurse loosens one of them and puts the swaddled baby in the crook of my arm.

Newborn babies can't see anything but light and shadows. I know that, but those wide, blue eyes are looking directly into my face. He seems intent, listening as I talk to him.

He is warm and still in my arms. Not crying. Listening to the sound of his mother's voice.

"My son," I venture.

"Your name is Romann. You are my fine little son."

I Was Fifteen, Pregnant, and Scared

Maybe my story will help someone like me

By MARY KENNY, as told to her by her daughter

I *got pregnant midway through my sophomore year of high school. On my sixteenth birthday I was just going into maternity clothes. This is my story.*

The father of my child was a guy in his early twenties. Why did I have sex with him? I guess I didn't think we would have sex. I didn't expect him to be interested in me. I was flattered that an "older man" would be interested. I knew you could get pregnant even if you had sex only once, but I thought, "It won't happen to me." I only had sex once with the father of my child.

When I suspected I was pregnant, I didn't tell my parents. I didn't know how. I mean, what do you say? Do you just sit at the dinner table and say, "Oh, by the way, I have some news . . ."?

Instead I told a couple of my best friends. They told me I'd better act fast and get an abortion. They said they could help me find a place and get me there. (We weren't even old enough to drive.) They'd even help me get the money to pay for it. I just didn't know what to do. So for a couple of weeks I did nothing.

I was upset, and it showed. I avoided my parents and stayed away from home. We had rules in our house, but I broke them. I didn't care. They didn't seem very important.

One night I came home hours past my curfew. My father was waiting up for me. I said I was going to bed.

"Come back here," he said. "Something is really wrong. Do you want to tell me what it is?"

"You're so smart. You know all the answers," I told him. "You tell me."

"I think you're pregnant," he said quietly.

I started to cry. I don't know how my parents found out. Maybe they just guessed. I was relieved that they knew.

I told him he was right. I was planning to get an abortion, and I might need his consent. I wanted to sound him out. My friends said I would not need parents' consent if I said I was eighteen. They told me all the girls do that and doctors expect it. They will write it down without questioning, so there would be no problem. I didn't know if I could do that, and I knew I couldn't even get a tetanus shot without my parents' consent, so I still wanted their response.

My dad hesitated. Finally he said, "You are a big girl with a big-girl problem. You have to make this decision yourself. If you do have an abortion, I won't kick you out or stop loving you. But abortion is contrary to everything I believe. I can't go against my deepest beliefs, not even to help you. There is no way I can help you get an abortion."

My father never preached to me. He never threatened me with sin or hell or anything like that. My parents are committed to us kids. They have spent their lives supporting and nurturing kids. That's what my father meant when he said abortion was contrary to all his beliefs. He didn't talk me out of an abortion that night, but I had a lot of doubts.

There was another influence in my life at that time that turned me away from abortion. My littlest brother was only about fifteen months old. I baby-sat and helped care for him. He reminded me of what babies were like. I didn't think of an anonymous "thing" inside me. I thought of a real baby like my little brother. When I thought that way, I couldn't see having an abortion.

Marriage was never a choice for me. I knew, quite honestly, that the baby's father did not care whether I lived or died. But I don't think I would have chosen marriage even if we had cared for each other. In my experience, the kids who have gotten married when they were sixteen or seventeen because the girl was pregnant have rarely had good marriages. One of my friends was pregnant and got married at seventeen. She was divorced at nineteen. Now at twenty she is trying to raise a three-year-old daughter alone while going to school. My pregnancy was a problem, but getting into a bad marriage would only have made things worse.

* * *

Once I gave up the idea of abortion, I relaxed a bit. I realized I had plenty of time to make a decision.

First I tried to find some way to keep my baby without taking full responsibility while I was still growing up myself. I thought of going to Stephen's Farm. Often just called "The Farm," it is a place in Summertown, Tennessee, where the members live a communal life and support themselves by farming. I heard that they would raise my child free of charge, and I could take it back anytime I wanted. That sounded great. Then I thought further. I would have to leave my child there at least five years because I wouldn't be ready to care for him until I was at least twenty-one. Then I would appear and take him away. It seemed like a terrible thing to do to a child.

My next idea was to have my family help me raise my child. My parents were willing to support any of my ideas except abortion. My mom was really with me in this. She says all moms would be if their daughters gave them the chance. She was willing to have both me and my child live at home, but she did say we would have to clarify some matters. The baby could not have two mothers. Either she would be in charge or I would, but we couldn't both be in charge. I was willing to let her raise my baby for a while. I wanted to continue in school, then maybe get a job.

But here I faced the same problem I had had with "The Farm." In five years, my mother and dad would have been like parents. Taking my child then would be like breaking up a home. I didn't see how I could do that to my child or my parents.

I became convinced that I could not be a parent without taking the responsibility for my own child. But I wanted to finish school. I wanted to travel and work and study. I was many years away from being able to assume responsibility for another person.

About this time I also chose a name for my child: Sunrise.

I began to think of adoption. I'm adopted myself, as are some of my brothers and sisters. It was an idea I was comfortable with.

I knew a little of what couples go through when they want to adopt. I knew how they were interviewed and their houses visited. I felt my child had a very good chance of getting a fine home through adoption. In fact, compared to what I could give Sunrise at this point, I felt this baby had a better future through adoption than with me.

Not everyone understood how I felt. I took plenty of abuse from my friends and from adults in our neighborhood. They accused me of "giving up your own flesh and blood." My parents got the same treatment from some of their acquaintances who thought I was irresponsible to give up my child. But I was beginning to think it was the most responsible thing I could do.

I went to see a social worker. She listened to me and didn't pressure me at all. Talking to her helped me to weigh the possibilities.

When I finally said that I did want to give my child up for adoption, she still said that there was no hurry. She told me that I would have some voice in what kind of home my child got. While she would not identify the prospective parents, she knew several families that had been approved for adoption. She would tell me about their ages, their occupations, their religion, and whether they had any other children. I could indicate which characteristics I wanted for my child. I picked a family that already had one child. I wanted to make sure my child grew up with at least one brother or sister. Completing all the paperwork early would help that family to have Sunrise right away.

In my case the father of the child did not have any say. He was not interested. We did have to locate him and get his consent, but this was no problem as he was glad to be rid of his responsibility. I think the father should have a say about the child if he is willing to take some responsibility. The father who is not willing to do this should not be able to obstruct the mother's decision.

I continued to go to school right up to the birth of my child. I did not want to quit school and just sit around for weeks, so as long as I felt good, I just kept going to school.

My mother believes that babies and childbirth are good things, no matter what the circumstances. She also believes that preparation for childbirth is important, so in the week before I was due, she taught me how to have a baby. We practiced relaxation and breathing, and I learned what to expect.

I started into labor during the night, and with my mother I went to the hospital in the early morning hours. She stayed with me throughout. Around nine in the morning I gave birth to an eight-pound boy. The labor was easy. I think that knowing what I was doing made the big difference.

Since I was alert during my labor, I saw my son as soon as he was born. I knew right away that he was a fine, healthy baby. After two days in the hospital, I went home. I left my baby behind.

The fourth day after the birth, I dropped by school just long enough to pick up my books and assignments. My mother drove me. On the way home I asked to stop at the hospital. The adoptive parents I had helped to choose were going to pick up Sunrise that afternoon. I wanted to see him one more time.

My mother and I went up to the maternity ward. The nurse brought Sunrise from the nursery. The nurse held him, and my mother held me, and I just looked at him and cried and cried.

Finally I told my mother I was ready to go. The nurse took Sunrise back to the nursery. My mother and I left. I never saw him again.

I told this all to you because maybe it will help a girl somewhere who is pregnant and scared. Maybe her friends will support her and understand a little better what she is going through.

I had to make some very tough decisions when I was only fifteen. As I tell you about them now, though, I know they were good decisions.

I finished high school and I have gone on to do many of the things I wanted to do with my life. I work to support myself, and I'm going to school, studying art and photography. I still want to travel, and there are many things I want to learn.

I know that marriage involves a serious commitment to a partner and to the children you might have. That commitment is right when you are ready. I was not ready for it at sixteen, and I am not ready for it now. I won't be ready for marriage until I can make that kind of commitment. Meanwhile, somewhere, there is a Sunrise. . . .

"They've Kidnaped Melissa!"

The note said we would never see our four-year-old daughter again

By JUDITH PRINCE

My mother was a Catholic, but she married outside the Church and my father wouldn't allow me to be brought up as a Catholic. Nevertheless, my mother saw to it that I had a good religious upbringing, and she also told me many stories about the Virgin Mary, stories I grew to love.

When I was twenty I married my childhood sweetheart, Kenneth, and went to live in Fort Lee, New Jersey. Our first child, Kenneth Junior, was born on my twenty-second birthday, and Richard arrived a year later. But then for four long years we had no more children. Both Ken and I wanted a little girl, so when God blessed us with Melissa, a blonde beauty, we were completely happy.

Until Melissa was four, we had nothing but the usual cuts and bruises to worry about. But then came the day that I will never forget.

Kenny and Richie, now nine and eight, were in school, and I had left Melissa with Mrs. Banks while I went shopping. Mrs. Banks was a childless widow who came twice a week to help with the cleaning and laundry. She was thoroughly dependable and loved Melissa almost as much as I did. But on this particular day, there was no Melissa running to greet me as I got out of the car. Instead, there was a hysterical Mrs. Banks shouting, "I can't find her anywhere! I've looked all over and I can't find her anywhere!"

I put down my groceries and grabbed her by the arms. "What are you talking about?" I demanded. "Where's Melissa?"

"She's gone, she's gone! I can't find her anywhere!"

I forced myself to be calm; two hysterical women could accomplish nothing. I led her into the kitchen, and sat down with her. Then I said sternly, "Now, Mrs. Banks, you'll have to control yourself and tell me exactly what happened."

She was shaking and crying, but with a great effort she said, "I was hanging out the clothes and Melissa was playing with her ball. When she went around to the front of the house I called out, 'Don't go out of the yard, love,' and she answered, 'No, Mrs. Banks,' and I finished with the clothes.

"But when I went around to the front, she wasn't there. I called and looked everywhere, and I went in the house and called her name and looked in all the rooms, and I couldn't find her! She's gone, they've kidnaped Melissa!"

A sharp pain cut through me. "Did you call the police?" I asked. "Did you check with the neighbors?"

"No," she said, "I was just going to when you drove up."

I jumped for the telephone. When the police came, I quickly repeated what Mrs. Banks had told me. They immediately rechecked the house and yard, and also the neighbors whom I had already called. Melissa was nowhere to be found.

I gave the police a careful description of my little girl, and also a picture of her, and they did whatever the police do in such cases, while I called Ken and told him what had happened.

When I look back on it now, I don't see how any of us lived through that first night. The boys finally cried themselves to sleep, but Ken and Mrs. Banks and I sat up in an agony of listening for the police or the kidnaper to phone. Dawn found us still sleepless, and praying that the mail would bring us news of our baby.

It did, but the letter we received was not at all what we had been expecting. Instead of a ransom demand, it was an announcement that our child would never come back to us! The letter was typed on cheap tablet paper and read:

"I have Melissa and she is safe and happy. She came to my car when I held up a little puppy for her to look at. She is playing with it now.

"I am going to keep her. It isn't fair for you to have three children when I never could have even one. Now that I have Melissa I am happy, and you still have two children so you can be happy, too.

"Don't try to find me. If you do I will kill Melissa and then kill myself."

The letter was signed "A Mother at Last," and postmarked the day before from Connecticut. This brought the FBI into the case. Meanwhile Ken and I appeared on television and begged the kidnaper to return Melissa. But nothing at all happened, except that the police received hundreds of letters and phone calls stating that Melissa had been seen in different cities all over the United States.

I could picture our little girl terror-stricken at being away from her mommy and daddy and brothers, and maybe being beaten because her kidnaper was afraid the neighbors would hear her crying.

A month went by and still there was no word of Melissa.

One night, in spite of the two pills I had taken, I couldn't sleep. Getting out of bed quietly so as not to wake Ken, I went into the living room. As I sat hopelessly weeping, the memory of a long-forgotten event came back.

I was about ten at the time and had injured my arm in a fall. Although my parents took me to several doctors, it didn't heal and was very painful. My mother was sick with worry. Finally she seemed to make up her mind to something, and the next day, when my father was at work, she told me that we were going someplace.

"Elaine, dear," she said, "this must be our little secret, and we must never tell Daddy because he wouldn't understand." We walked to the Catholic church, and went in and up to the altar. When I saw the statue of God's Mother, looking so serene and holy, I fell to my knees without being told. Mother lit a candle, and then knelt down beside me.

We both prayed to Mary to heal my arm. In a week, it was entirely well.

I had completely forgotten this incident over the years, but now my heart filled with hope for the first time since Melissa had been kidnaped. "Mary will help me," I kept telling myself. "She understands the suffering of all mothers." The next morning I hurriedly dressed and drove to the Catholic church.

When I reached the altar and looked on Mary's face, the awe I remembered from my childhood swept over me again. I lit a candle, sank to my knees, and prayed to the Virgin to bring Melissa back to me.

All that day I seemed to be in a vacuum of waiting. I felt no sorrow, no emotion of any kind, only anticipation. And that evening, as we sat in the living room trying to comfort each other, we heard a banging on the door. When we rushed to open it, Melissa ran in crying, "Mommy, Mommy, Daddy, Daddy!" I leave you to imagine the joy that filled our hearts.

There was a note pinned to our darling's jacket. "I don't know what came over me," it read, "but this morning I got the feeling that I had to bring Melissa back. So here she is."

The Fischers:
Nine Children and
Four Races

"God made them for us, and He likes lots of colors!"

By ANNE BUCKLEY

A customer in a shoe store once eyed Eileen Fischer's large family and remarked, "I can't understand how anybody can love somebody else's child."

It is easy to see that Eileen and Bob Fischer are not the natural parents of their nine children. Five of the youngsters are of black parentage, two are Koreans, one has American Indian blood. Only one, Patty, twelve, is Caucasian.

But Eileen says firmly that "they are our children." She explains. "God made them for us, but sent them to us through other people."

And Bob shakes off compliments from people who call them a wonderful couple for "taking in all those children." Says he, "We don't see ourselves as wonderful. We see ourselves as fortunate. They are beautiful children."

And indeed they are, in the homey setting of the Fischer house in Hillsdale, New Jersey; each of them, from Francis, fifteen, down to John, who's pushing three. But on the adoption market, their vital statistics might seem less than desirable.

Francis, who is part American Indian, has a deformity and wears a brace. Mary, eight, who came from Korea with her sister, Elizabeth, nine, is blind. Stacey, ten; Joseph, eight; Tommy, six; and John are interracial. Christopher, five, is all black.

The Fischers are convinced that their vocation is to be the parents of hard-to-place children. They did not plan it that way. They were married only a year and a half when, after Eileen had had a few miscarriages, they learned of the need for adoptive parents for physically handicapped children. Their first application brought them Francis. Next came Patty. When they adopted Stacey, they were not specifically bent on proving something about racial harmony. "We *wanted* the baby," explains Eileen. That Stacey was a black-Irish mixture was immaterial.

But now they perceive that their family is a kind of proving ground for the principle that prejudice is not innate. "A family like ours opens you up," says Bob. "After the fall of Saigon, the kids wanted us to adopt half of Vietnam. When we explained the reasons why we couldn't at the time, they started naming neighbors who could take children—placing them all over town."

There appear to be no sticky subjects in the Fischer household. Eileen fondles Christopher's head and giggles. "A black woman stopped me one day and explained how to do his hair, but I haven't learned it yet. It takes so long," she says.

The whole family laughs about the night, after lights out, when a voice was heard reading a story to the others. It was little Mary, using her Braille skills in the darkness.

And another family story is of the judge at one of the adoption proceedings who looked at fair-haired Patty amid the dark-skinned brood, and reduced her to tears with the question, "How did you get into this group?" Quips Bob: "She's our token honky."

Among the Fischers, what other people would consider a handicap is turned to an advantage. Francis, with his artificial leg, is a dance contest winner bent on an acting career. He played in the cast of the musical *Li'l Abner* at his high school. Mary stars in a film made by the Commission for the Blind.

Elizabeth tells a visitor that Mary is her favorite among all her sisters and brothers, "because she was my sister in Korea." But Mary is a favorite all around; Bob Fischer explains, "It's not her blindness, it's her personality; she's sweet. Our handicapped children, we've found, are the brightest, most socially adjusted."

Elizabeth remembers well the twenty-five-hour plane ride from Korea four years ago; the feeling of being "ascared"; the worry on landing that "a fat lady standing there" was her new mother and her relief when it turned out to be Eileen; the delight of meeting not only her five brothers and sisters but also her grandmother, Mrs. Madeline Fischer, a member of the household. She also remembers harrowing details of her early life with Mary, whom she served as a fiercely protective little mother when the tots were abandoned.

Each Fischer child knows something of his or her background. Tommy, for example, is aware that he had a Jewish parent as well as a black one, and the rest of the kids get a kick out of wishing him a happy Hanukkah. "Whatever information we have belongs to them," says Eileen. "If someday they want to track down their natural parents, that's fine with me. We're not threatened by that." Says Bob, "When they ask a question, we answer it."

Bob Fischer is accustomed to answering questions. He is a special education teacher who headed the Rockland County Special Education Instructional Materials Center at the county Board of Cooperative Educational Services. He is also a permanent deacon, ordained with the Newark Archdiocese's first diaconal class, and assigned to St. John's parish, where all the grade-school Fischers are students.

Bob became a Catholic at age twenty-two in 1955, and was followed into the Church by his mother and father. He sought out the diaconate as a natural next step in his spiritual progress. Although the training program was demanding ("We adopted four children in two years in the middle of it"), he finds that his ministry and his family life mesh smoothly. Eileen often accompanies him on his visits to people in the hospital; and the children take turns going along on the house visits, much to the delight of the shut-ins.

Bob and Eileen have been involved in the charismatic renewal movement for seven years and recently began a prayer group in their own parish. They pray with their children, too, often with joined hands in their "love circle" around a lighted candle.

Bob remembers that his reception into the Church occurred on March 19, the feast of St. Joseph. "At the time I would have preferred a more cerebral saint—Thomas Aquinas, for example," he says. "But isn't it significant that like St. Joseph my vocation is to be a foster father?"

Bob, an only child himself, works at the role of father. Each Saturday one member of the family is taken out to lunch with Daddy, alone, for one-to-one attention. The schedule ranges from baby John through Mother, Eileen, and Grandmother.

The adornments of the Fischer house are simple and tell a great deal about the values of the people who live there: small banners on the porch with slogans like "The whole world is a joyous happening to those who love"; an old church pew to accommodate a row of children; a floral arrangement surviving from Grandma's birthday.

They manage with only one car. Something has always come up when they were on the point of buying a second: Francis' leg surgery; Mary's corneal transplant (which was unsuccessful but will be tried again when she is a little older); emergency surgery last summer for Eileen, who faces another hospitalization some time soon. But the lack of a second car is turned to an asset: it gives them, they explain, the opportunity to experience the love and kindness of others who offer a needed ride to a doctor's office or supermarket.

The Fischers once extended their hospitality for six months to an unwed mother-to-be. For them, it was no big thing, except that Bob confesses to being "a nervous wreck" during the midnight drive to the hospital for the delivery—something, this father of nine points out, he'd never gone through before.

The only time a note of harshness creeps into the conversation of Eileen and Bob Fischer is when they address the subject of abortion. Bob deplores the fact that though Catholics lead the crusade against abortion, few come forward as adoptive parents of the children delivered by black unwed mothers. But Eileen feels that "there are plenty of people would could adopt these children—handicapped, racially mixed—if the mothers would only be unselfish enough to deliver them."

The Fischers consider themselves specially graced by God for their particular style of family life, and do not expect others to do what they are doing. But they often help couples who are considering adoption. Five of their own children came through the New Jersey Department of Youth and Family Services, the two Koreans through the Holt International Children's Service, and the last two through Associated Catholic Charities. And if their example encourages others to seek out a special child, they are delighted.

"Our family is a reflection of God the Father's love for his children," says Bob. "We represent the People of God, mankind. That's not extraordinary—it's the normal thing." God, he adds with a smile, "likes lots of colors."

VII

COURAGE
OF
THE HANDICAPPED
AND THEIR
LOVED ONES

"Rosemary Brought Us Strength"

*And her handicap indirectly improved the lot of the
retarded all over the United States*

By ROSE KENNEDY

I am often asked, "Mrs. Kennedy, how can you go on in the face of all the tragedy that has befallen you?" I believe it is a matter of will; God's will and my will.

Early in life I decided that I would not be overcome by events. Life is not easy for any of us. But it is a continual challenge, and it is up to us to be cheerful and strong so that those who depend on us may draw strength from our example.

When I discovered that my daughter Rosemary was retarded, my first reaction was shocked surprise. Like all mothers, I had prayed that my child would be born normal and healthy.

In the birth of my two oldest sons, Joe and Jack, this prayer had been answered. But now we went from doctor to doctor seeking hope. From all, we heard the same answer: "I'm sorry, but we can do nothing." For my husband and me it was nerve-wracking and incomprehensible.

We were comforted then, as so often in our lives, by the magnificent "Meditation" written by John Henry Cardinal Newman, the nineteenth-century English convert and author. "God has created me to do Him some definite service," he wrote. "He has committed some work to me which He has not committed to another. I have my mission. I may never know it in this life, but I shall be told it in the next. I am a link in a chain, a bond of connection between persons. He has not created me for naught. I shall do good. If I am in sickness, my sickness may serve Him; in perplexity, my perplexity may serve Him; if I am in sorrow, my sorrow may serve Him. He does nothing in vain. He may throw me among strangers. He may make me feel desolate, make my spirit sick, hide my future from me, still He knows what He is about.''

Rosemary was born at home, a normal delivery. She was a beautiful child. But she was slower to crawl, slower to walk and speak than her two brothers. I was told she would catch up later, but she never did.

The presence of Rosemary in our family was a constant illumination. Though we tried to treat Rosemary the same as the others, our children seemed to sense her great need for compassion, and they willingly gave it.

They tried to include Rosemary in everything they did. At Hyannis Port she would crew in their boat races; she usually could help with the jib or hold the mainsheet. Winning at anything always brought a marvelous smile to her face.

She was always one of the team and it was accepted and understood by the other children that Rosemary did not go sailing or swimming alone. She did what they did, even to taking tennis lessons. She loved dances. When she went to a dance Jack would take her card and fill out some of her dances for her with his friends. I know it wasn't easy for them, especially when Rosemary would say, ''Why don't other boys ask me to dance?''

I am sure that my sons and daughters acquired much of their desire to help the less fortunate from their experience with Rosemary. When some of them were later in a position to influence public opinion and to shape policy, the lesson Rosemary taught them influenced the lives of handicapped people everywhere.

Parents ask me whether all mentally retarded children should be kept at home. I do not think a simple answer can apply to all. Certainly there is no substitute for the physical and emotional stimulation that a mother and father (and brothers and sisters) can give a child, especially in the first year or two of life. But just as there came a time when we felt Rosemary would benefit from being away from home, so every family may have to face not being able to care for their child.

Fortunately, we have traveled far from the days when the only alternative to home was a large, impersonal institution. In a growing number of states laws have established the right of every handicapped child to complete public education.

There is a growing acceptance of mental and physical differences.

The retarded are far more like other people than they are different from them. And even the differences are no longer perceived as threatening.

When parents of handicapped children ask me for advice, here is what I tell them.

1. Often we can help prevent mental retardation. We can test for the mental disease phenylketonuria and control it by diet. We can vaccinate against the subtle danger to babies, German measles. We now know the cause of mongolism, and perhaps in the near future, we'll be able to cure it. And we are aware that as much as 75 percent of all mental retardation is induced by poverty, poor medical care, inadequate diet, lack of affection and stimulation; not by genetic defect or birth accident.

2. All children are different. Some are short, some tall, some black, some white. Some children do not hear or see or walk or talk as well as other children. Some do not learn as quickly. None of these differences is cause for shame or guilt.

3. Despite these differences, children can be loved: not only by their families but also by the people of their community.

4. *A handicapped child can actually strengthen a family.* Research has shown that such children often deepen the love between brothers and sisters, husbands and wives.

5. *More than eighty percent of the mentally retarded learn to read, sing, respond, and grasp life with eagerness and joy.* And handicapped children will try even harder when they are praised or rewarded. Every time I would say, "Rosemary, you have the best teeth and smile in the family," she would smile for hours. She liked to wear pretty clothes, have her hair fixed, and her fingernails polished. Even if I said to her no more than "Rosemary, that's the most beautiful hair ribbon," she would be thrilled.

I tell parents that as their retarded children grow older, they will find even greater understanding and help in training them to participate in the community.

Before Jack became president, no retarded person could get a job in the federal government. Civil service regulations limited government jobs to those scoring more than a certain I.Q. Jack had this regulation stricken, and now more than 20,000 retarded men and women are employed in the various branches of government. Some of them earn

$10,000 to $15,000 a year. More than 600 have received awards for outstanding performance.

My husband and I established the Joseph Kennedy, Jr., Foundation almost thirty years ago* in honor of our departed oldest son, Joe. In 1968 the foundation created the "Special Olympics" and still sponsors it. The games invite more than 400,000 boys and girls from all over the world to compete with each other each year. In 15,000 local meets and tournaments they take part in track and field, basketball, swimming, volleyball, bowling, ice skating, and many other events.

My vision, and I hope yours, is a world in which mental retardation, like polio, will be almost entirely eradicated. Then and only then can we say, in the words of St. Paul, "I have fought the good fight. I have finished the course. I have kept the faith."

*At the time this article was first published.

Andrew, My Special Brother

My parents need not have worried about his effect on my growing up—there was some pain but much pride

By JENNIFER BLAKE

I was nine years old when Mom and Dad told me that my only brother, Andrew, then nineteen, was retarded. (I am not using our real names.) I remember at the time that I was not sure what the term meant. I was the only other child in the family, and my parents could not tell what effect Andrew's condition would have on me. It certainly didn't become for me any emotional trauma. I had suspected something was different about him, but when actually faced with the fact, I accepted the whole matter just as it was.

The thought of my finding someone to blame it on never entered my mind. I think for a short while I looked at him with curiosity, now that a medical term had been attached to things. However, the curiosity wore off in a few days. After all, as far as a nine-year-old was concerned, he was still the same big brother he had been before.

In Andrew the signs of brain damage didn't show until he started school. One day he came home with a test marked zero. After a few more similar tests with the same results, Andrew was taken to a doctor for examinations.

His had been a difficult birth, but no one had known how difficult until he was six. The result was brain damage, due to lack of oxygen to one area of the brain. Recent tests have shown his IQ now to be around 70, mildly retarded.

By the time Andrew was in the second grade Mom and Dad could see that their son would never be able to go beyond special education classes. They didn't let this discovery stand in the way of their love and hopes for my brother. There was no pity, nor were there thoughts of sheltering him away from the world, because they believed that, as a human being, he had the right to experience the things that other people did.

I was born when Andrew was ten. Mom later told me that he would sit for hours quietly watching the crib. When I was put outside in the playpen, he would guard the backyard like a hawk, making sure that nothing was going to harm his sister. This was the beginning of the years of devotion and love that only a special brother could have for a younger sister.

The ten years' difference in age between us never seemed a gap. In the beginning, when I was small, we were nearly always together. Right from the start both of us were extroverts, yet each in his own way. The beautiful thing was that we were never competing for attention from anyone.

Andrew could charm a cookie from any woman on the block. Naturally his younger sister trailed along behind him, mooching some of his treasures.

Andrew's speech is understandable, though not always clear. If he gets excited his thoughts get ahead of his words and we ask him to slow down, which he does. He never hesitates to enter a conversation and it does not have to be "brought down" to his level because he follows along quite well.

He never hesitated to share any of his things, whether it was a chocolate bar or a baseball. I believe that this is one of the most beautiful qualities of these special people. The ability to share and give is something we can all learn. Typical of today's retarded children, and of Andrew when he was younger, is the ability to make small things, which normal children and even adults ignore, into objects of beauty and meaning.

Andrew didn't and still doesn't believe in fighting. Rarely did the need to fight ever arise, because he got on well with the other children. I can remember vividly one time when Andrew had to take a stand against another boy, and of course he did it for his younger sister.

In most neighborhoods, there is usually at least one boy generally regarded as a bully. Our neighborhood was no exception, and it was this boy that my brother stood up to. He was extremely small for his age at the time, and I will never forget watching him step in front of me with fists clenched and order that boy to either fight or leave. Perhaps the other boy was taken by surprise at the outburst from our usually sunny-tempered Andrew, or maybe it was the look of determination that he saw on his face, but anyway he left and never bothered us again.

When Andrew was sixteen, he was transferred to another school where special classes were held for slow children. It was here that he learned carpentry and woodworking and simple reading, writing, and arithmetic. His letters to me today are original and descriptive. He goes into extraordinary detail and writes with good humor.

It was here, too, that he met many boys like himself who became his close friends. Even now, twelve years later, two of his best friends are still with him from those school days.

At nineteen, Andrew left school and got a job in a factory. His employer was a man with a large heart, who understood what this meant not only to my brother but to my parents, too. Quickly Andrew won the hearts of those in the small factory and today they lovingly call him the "president of the plant." Never was there a brighter day than when he came charging into the house waving his first paycheck. Receiving your first paycheck, no matter who you are, is a pretty important thing, so you can imagine what it meant to my brother.

One can think of many things one would like to do with the money. Andrew, too, thought of all these things. It was a pretty proud young man who walked up to the cashier and paid the bill for a delicious meal for our family. It came out of that first check.

The innocence of children can sometimes be an illusion rather than a reality. When I was in the 8th grade, one boy who knew my brother and his friends tried to show off a little by spreading nasty stories about how stupid the boys were and what a crazy family I must have. His stories were nasty, but my aim was nastier, and he found himself on the ground following a left jab from me.

The whole matter blew over quickly at school and the boy kept his mouth shut on the playground from then on. What was left for me after that was a new feeling, a sense of confusion about my brother. It was the beginning of a period of doubt that lasted nearly three years, tearing Andrew and me apart. I became obsessed with the fear that I would lose friends because of him.

I suppose it would sound better for me if I didn't put this part into the story. However, if I left this out, it wouldn't be a true account of my thoughts and feelings. I will have to admit that, after the incident at school, I felt some shame and embarrassment in my relationship with Andrew. I suppose that every young person with a brain-damaged brother or sister feels at one time or another the way I did.

Secretly, and sometimes openly, I began to rip my brother apart. I felt that my parents were always comparing me with Andrew because "Andrew was the perfect child when he was younger."

Of course, they weren't really doing this, but I believed it at the time. When I was punished for doing something that Andrew had nothing to do with, I usually came back at him to relieve my frustration and anger. I used to get so exasperated when he didn't understand something or he couldn't do a certain thing the right way.

Very clearly I recall the times I used to ask God to make my brother right, or the way I wanted him to be. I knew it would take a pretty big miracle, but I was stubborn and determined not to settle for anything less. As the days turned into weeks, then months, and finally years, my patience slowly ebbed. Little did I realize the near miracle that God would soon perform, not with Andrew but with me.

With regret I can remember the times I convinced my friends that we should go to their house instead of mine because I knew Andrew was home. Nor will I forget the times I spent in tears at night wishing that I had a big brother I could talk to, like other girls had.

I was not consoled that Andrew does not *look* retarded. He has dark brown hair, wears glasses, and he is slim and about six feet tall. His features are young-looking, so that even now, at twenty-eight, he looks like someone in his late teens.

Once during this time there was an instance where I forgot my anger and frustration and saw Andrew as a person with a need. After Andrew had been working at the factory for five years, my parents were told that part of the plant, the part my brother worked in, would be moving to a new city. It was pretty tense around the house as my parents tried to decide whether Andrew should go with the factory or leave it in the hope of getting another job. In the end it was decided he should go with the plant.

After a couple of moves, Andrew was settled in with a couple who ran a boarding house outside the new city. I will never forget the first few weeks after he left. Everything was so quiet, and the meals didn't seem complete without the fourth member of our family.

It was evident that Andrew missed us, but he quickly won a very special place in the hearts of the couple who took him in, and they treated him like a second son. Their home soon became his home.

After a short while, though, Andrew found that, because their house was so far out, he could not enjoy events that occurred in town in the evenings after work. Thus, with regret, our family searched for a new boarding place. Naturally the couple felt bad about Andrew's leaving them but they wanted him to be happy.

Andrew moved into a new boarding place within the city limits and began to learn something about life outside our home.

But trouble started with a phone call to our house a few weeks later. The woman owner of the boarding house said that Andrew could not live with them because he was disturbing the other boys.

No one could believe such a thing could be true. Andrew willingly helped her with dishes and other household chores. He never told us about the way he was treated until after he found out that he would not have to go back there again. For once I forgot my coldness toward my brother as I raged against anyone who could be so cruel.

When his "second parents" heard about the incident, they immediately offered their home and love once more. Andrew gratefully accepted and continued to live there until the plant moved back to our city three years later. Today, he is still working at the same plant, putting in regular hours from 8 A.M. to 4 P.M.

By living away from those he loved, my brother did what I feel is the hardest thing a mentally retarded person can do. This experience made my brother grow a little older, as he learned to assume more responsibilities not only toward himself but toward other people around him.

With Andrew back at home for good, I remember that I had mixed feelings. Of course I was glad to see him fill his rightful place at mealtimes. On the other hand, the embarrassment returned. I knew that I was wrong and I felt guilty about it, but the feelings were stronger than the guilt and I made no real effort to correct myself.

Then, one beautiful night, I came to realize that I really did have a big brother. I saw that I had more than most girls have, for he is not just a brother, but a very special one at that.

The night I came to this conclusion I was on the way home from seven tremendous days in Jamaica. Ever since I was a baby, our family had traveled by car extensively through Canada and a good part of the United States. For our last trip before I left for college we flew down to Jamaica.

While we were there I watched and waited apprehensively to see if Andrew would do what he usually did. Someone could be standing at a bus stop and Andrew could walk up and start a conversation. Guaranteed, within about three minutes they would be talking like old friends. Sure enough, we had hardly got settled in the hotel and seated by the pool when he was stopping to talk at the tables. Oh, I can remember how this used to drive me absolutely crazy when he did this on our other trips.

Yet this time I forced myself to stay and watch the reactions of the people. To my amazement, they seemed to love the friendliness of my brother. I began to think that perhaps I was a little hasty in my judgment of him. But it was on the flight home that I knew how wrong I had been for the past few years. So many people, his new-found friends, wanted him to come and talk with them that he was hardly in his seat the whole way home.

Back home in my own bed that night, I lay awake thinking for a long time. What God didn't give my brother in brains, He made up for in heart. Andrew's heart knows no hate but sees each person as a human being with feelings like his own. Whether a person is rich or poor, black, white, or red, makes no difference, for his love is able to take in everyone.

To those around him, Andrew gives understanding without hypocrisy, friendship without prejudice, and love without reserve. He has never told me that he loves me. He has never given me a brotherly hug. But these things are insignificant because he knows that I am there and he believes that I understand our relationship. Now I do.

I cried that night and many nights since then, not with tears of sorrow but with tears of joy. On that night I found Andrew. I discovered that my love for my brother goes deeper than what other people may think or say.

My brother will never be a doctor or lawyer. He will never win the Nobel prize in science. He will never be known throughout the world as a statesman. But those who come in contact with Andrew, and the many who are like him, will experience the joy and happiness that these beautiful people have in giving their gift of love day by day.

I am thankful, for I, too, have been given the opportunity to experience these feelings. I wish that every person will some day come to know and love someone like my special kind of brother.

All God's Children

Todd was just one of dozens of youngsters, healthy and handicapped, in our family—but his story is a special one

By DOROTHY GAUCHAT

How had we—Bill and Dorothy Gauchat—ever gotten ourselves into this sort of thing? What on earth had caused us to agree to care for another poor, hopeless creature? Nothing on earth, we would have been forced to answer. Our first glimpse of each other—Bill and I—had come in the depths of the Depression. With a couple of other school girls, I had visited Bill's Hospitality House, an abandoned store which Bill had made into a haven for the unfortunates who roamed the city.

No doubt Bill and I were crazy eventually to marry each other. Some people were saying that the way the country was going anybody was crazy to marry anybody and to bring children into the world. But young people are forever optimistic and adventurous.

So there we were, a few years later, with five children of our own. Four were normal, healthy, lovely youngsters.

Anita, the busy practical one. Small and wiry, her brown braids bouncing as she flew here and there, issuing orders, thinking up games to play.

Helenmarie. Golden hair, blue eyes, a dreamy disposition, and a bottomless store of questions with which to tax her parents' patience.

Susie, blue-eyed, brown-haired, playful; and Eric, big, blond, and full of bounce.

Our fourth girl, Colette, had shown alarming symptoms of brain damage as a toddler. Then mysteriously (and, we were to learn, temporarily), the symptoms had cleared up.

Then there were David and Robin, our two foster children. David had come to us at six months, blind, deaf, hydrocephalic, with a spinal lesion. But he had recovered, surprising doctors and amazing his parents. Baby Robin was a victim of total cerebral palsy, and subject to sudden respiratory infections. One of these had almost killed him, but lately he seemed to be improving.

And now we were faced with Todd.

On a day in late summer, a young man had come to our door carrying a small boy. He had heard that we had taken handicapped children into our home, and he introduced us to his son Todd. He explained to me —and to the children, who had gathered around—that two-year-old Todd had cerebral palsy. He needed a home.

Todd looked famished. His arms and legs, pitifully thin, thrashed out uncontrollably. He was tiny (thirteen pounds) but he had the face of an older child.

I wanted to cry with pity. Then I saw his eyes. They were deep brown, brimming with intelligent interest. And he looked at me with a wholehearted smile.

Our children clustered about Todd as his father put him on the floor. He took in the strange surroundings and strange faces. He saw a newspaper across the room, and set his jaw in determination. His body jerked and edged its way toward his goal. The children wanted to get the paper for him, but his father stopped them, and told them to watch.

Todd was straining every muscle and nerve, but his face was aglow with challenge. He reached his goal, beads of perspiration covering his face and dampening his brown hair. He gurgled with glee, waving the crumpled paper like a flag of victory.

We were all caught up in the excitement of this diminutive hero's achievement. There was something contagious about his joyful determination. And Todd seemed to enjoy the attention. As he and the children played, his father drew me aside and explained again Todd's need for a home. But the talk of caring for another child seemed impossible.

It was hard to turn the young man away; he seemed to have more than his share of heartaches. The children frowned their disapproval at me. They wanted to keep Todd. I was grateful that we were blessed with happy, generous kids. Their hearts and home were open to everybody and everything. A week hardly passed when one didn't come home with an injured bird, a stray kitten, a puppy.

But we couldn't keep Todd. Holding him in my lap I could feel his ribs. He was pitifully thin. Yet he possessed a hidden spring of vitality. I loved him. My words of refusal to his father must have sounded hollow. They were.

As Bill's car came into the driveway that evening, the children raced to see who could reach him first. The winner was Anita, the oldest of all.

"And Daddy," she said, "we'll help Mom take care of him. Please say we can have him." The others joined in the chorus of pleas.

To say Bill was a bit overwhelmed would be an understatement. He said to me, "It looks like another snow job."

As we sat out under the stars that evening at the side of our little lake, I gave Bill the details of the day. I tried to be realistic and practical about the little boy. But I realized, after talking with Bill, that I badly wanted to add Todd to our family.

For the next few weeks, thoughts of Todd occupied my mind. I had heard of a woman in the village who did day work. Perhaps if I hired her a day or two a week, I would have time for another child. Besides, our girls were a big help with dishes, and cared for their own rooms.

Bill reminded me that I had already told Todd's father that I could not care for the boy. By now the little fellow was probably settled safely in a new home. The incident was closed.

The days were growing shorter, and the children had returned to school. The house had taken on a comparative quiet and a new order. One evening as the children were gathered around the table in the kitchen, working at school assignments, the telephone bell disturbed the industrious silence. I did not recognize the caller's voice at first, until he mentioned Todd.

"Do you think you could reconsider taking Todd? I haven't been able to find a home for him."

"Let me discuss it with my husband. I'll call you back tomorrow."

Everyone was watching as I ended the conversation. To Bill I said: "How about a quick walk around the yard? It's a beautiful night, and a beautiful moon."

"As soon as I get my pipe," he said.

As we walked through the dried leaves, Bill took a long time lighting his pipe, waiting for me to begin.

"It was Todd's father," I said finally. "He can't find a home for him. He wants to know if we would take Todd."

"*Que sera sera*, whatever will be will be." Bill was humming softly as I talked.

"You know the children have the right idea," I said, "the Christian spirit of hospitality. Remember how at the Hospitality House we welcomed everyone? At first the neighbors complained about the 'bums and tramps,' and the police sent health inspectors who complained about the chipped cups and cracked bowls. And you told them a hungry man was kept from starvation by what was in those cracked and chipped dishes."

"Right, let's keep up the spirit of hospitality. We'll take Todd."

We shared a quiet smile. In the October moonlight it was settled. We decided not to tell the children; we'd surprise them.

It was a brilliant autumn day when Todd arrived. For Todd, I'm afraid, it wasn't a happy day. He watched with apprehension as his father assembled his bed. He was frightened. He didn't want to come to me. He lay on the floor close to his father.

He looked pitiful and scrawny. His head was bald in patches: evidently someone had attempted to give him a haircut. Doing that for a spastic child is an unnerving job, we later learned from experience.

After finishing the bed, Todd's father lifted him in his arms and settled down in a big chair. Quietly he tried to explain to the boy why he was leaving him with a new family.

He promised to visit Todd often; the boy fought back tears, but it was too much. He buried his small head on his father's chest and sobbed in utter misery.

I motioned to his father to give him to me. "Perhaps," I said, "it would be best to leave. It will take a little time for him to adjust."

Todd's body was rigid with fear. His thin frame was convulsed with his sobbing. I tried to walk with him. Finally I settled into my favorite old rocking chair beside Robin's bed. Gradually the boy's twisted body relaxed, and he nestled closer as I rocked and purred soft nonsense into his ear.

We went on rocking and all the while Todd's brown eyes looked up at me. "How would you like a little milk?" I asked. I didn't expect an answer (I suppose I was almost as frightened as he), but he nodded vigorously. I placed him in his bed and went to the kitchen to prepare a bottle.

His father had said he could drink from a bottle, but that he had difficulty with it, and also with solid foods. We learned gradually that what went into his mouth did not always stay there. A sudden spasm would reject the food and I had to start over again. But he loved food, and any sight or mention of it brought him to full attention.

With the warmed bottle in my hand, Todd and I resumed our rocking. Now his hungry mouth grabbed the nipple. He choked and sputtered. Milk dribbled from the side of his mouth. It was painful to watch his hungry effort; he'd stop momentarily to catch his breath though he seemed fearful that I might take the bottle from him. I felt myself growing tense and exhausted along with him. We needed no words for communication.

It was hard to imagine anyone so hungry, and so helpless to meet the need. I realized how much we take for granted—walking, talking, eating, drinking, relaxing; this child could do none of these ordinary, natural things.

Finally Todd swallowed the last drop of milk and slumped exhaustedly in my arms. Sweat ran down his forehead and cheeks.

I heard the school bus stop out in front. Sue appeared first at the door. "Oh, Mommy!" she cried as her eyes settled on Todd. She rushed to the bed and knelt beside us. "You did take him! You did take him!"

The weeks passed swiftly, tranquilly, and Todd's bony body filled out. His skin took on a bronze glow, replacing the dehydrated pallor of a malnourished child. The long, patient hours with him were showing results. His older sisters were proud of their skill in feeding him. Love, as much as the food in his bottle, was needed to get nourishment into that shrunken body.

Todd's cerebral palsy affected the upper part of his body; hence he could not control the movement of his arms or balance his body in a sitting position. His head jerked, and the muscles of his throat involuntarily constricted, making it impossible for him to swallow until the muscles relaxed. Although he never became discouraged as he "slurped" away, he surely did become exhausted. Often after his intense struggle he fell asleep in my arms, his clothing damp with perspiration.

He seemed to be chronically hungry, always on the lookout for an extra snack. He spent hours with us in the kitchen watching the family in action. He sat in a narrow chair designed for spastics; it could be tilted back to keep his body from falling forward. It had been given to him by the local Cerebral Palsy Society.

As I prepared meals, Todd would open his mouth wide like a young bird in its nest. When I took a spoon and medicine bottle for Robin, Todd opened for a share of it.

We added eggs and honey to whole milk to give him as much nourishment as possible. Not only did his body thrive, but his damaged spirit also.

The response of our younger son David to his new brother was a joy to watch. After asking endless questions about Todd's condition, David accepted the difference and adopted Todd as his playmate.

The two spent hours on the living room floor playing with trucks and trains, building forts, and having noisy, make-believe battles. David had an uncanny way of communicating with Todd. There was immediate rapport between them. If Todd couldn't handle a toy, David did it for him; he was quick to notice Todd's needs.

At other times, Todd was content to spend long hours watching his playmate. David loved to draw and make things even at this early age; he had a flair for creative crafts. Todd didn't seem to mind that he couldn't use his hands to join in, but only sat back, his face glowing with admiration at David's triumphs.

As the months and years passed, Todd's progress was remarkable. He went twice a week for physical and speech therapy at the Cerebral Palsy Rehabilitation Center, ten miles from home. The orthopedic specialist and therapists gave encouraging reports. They enjoyed working with Todd because he was so cooperative and determined.

He was fitted with steel braces from shoulders to toes; encased in these, he could stand erect at his table, and could hold his otherwise jerking and drooping body straight as he sat in his wheelchair. All this iron made it awkward to dress him, though. We looked forward to the day when he could stand and sit without braces, perhaps even walk.

Bill constructed a set of parallel bars, and between them Todd struggled to move his rigid body step by step. It was agonizing to watch him concentrate and try to control his hands, in order not to lose his grip on the bars. He needed every ounce of his energy to try to make his whole body work together.

It exhausted me merely to watch him: beads of sweat rolled down his face; his lower lip was thrust out with bulldog tenacity as he sought to will order on his disorganized reflexes.

Todd was no quitter; whenever he lost his grip and pitched forward, he would look up from the floor with a big grin and nod when asked if he wanted to try again.

He had a small tricycle to which we welded a solid steel back brace which encircled his chest to hold him upright. With his feet strapped to the pedals, he would try to wheel about the house.

Here again, when he had control of one limb, the opposite leg or arm would strike out in reverse. He would weave in every direction, banging into furniture.

All this activity was a part of Todd's therapy to strengthen his muscles and coordinate his movements. With each piece of equipment, our expectations rose as though each were a magic wand which would enable him to walk or run. We were sometimes impatient with his physical progress, but the doctors and therapists reassured us.

"It takes a long time with cerebral palsy," they said, and Todd would grin and grind his teeth in a show of determination. Actually, though, the harder he tried the more tense he got. The more tense he got the more spastic and helpless he became. Gradually, we learned from watching him that the secret to success was relaxing.

Over and over again I'd say, "Relax, take a deep breath. Make yourself feel like an old rag doll and then try again." This was hard for Todd to do. He was in a hurry for success.

The crisis came on a day in June when Todd was seven. When Bill returned from work that evening, I met him at the door. I was in a kind of shock.

The caseworker was here this afternoon. They were going to take Todd away and put him in the state school for the mentally retarded.

Todd was still very spastic. He could not speak or sit or stand unassisted.

He had continued to make weekly trips to the rehabilitation center for therapy sessions. And on one of these visits a county psychologist had given him an I.Q. test. The result accorded with the plan of Child Welfare to place Todd in the state school. We had never thought of this possibility, because Todd was mentally normal.

Through questioning, we learned that the so-called intelligence test given to Todd was a standard test for a normal child of his age group.

"How," we asked, "can he answer questions when he can't speak? How can he place blocks when he has no control of his hands? In short, how could any fair-minded practitioner of psychometric evaluations claim that such a test indicated this child's intelligence? The most it could prove was that the child was physically unable to participate in such tests."

The answers we received to these objections skirted the issue. They ranged from acts of blind faith tests, to an observation that we were emotionally involved.

Of course we were emotionally involved! We loved Todd. We also were intelligent enough to observe facts and draw reasonable conclusions. Although love is called blind, it very often gives deep, revealing insights.

As foster parents, however, we were helpless. We pleaded with Todd's social worker at least to allow us to be present at a testing, so that we could interpret for him. But every appeal fell on deaf ears. In a few months a deputy sheriff would drive up to take Todd away.

It was then that we grasped the hope of making Todd our legal son.

No one knew better than we did the enormous life responsibility we would be taking on. We considered carefully, weighing our responsibility to our own children, as well as our love for Todd. Then we decided.

As delicately as we could, we suggested adoption to Todd's father. He approved. He had been unemployed for over a year. And he told us that Todd had been baptized a Catholic immediately after birth, when it appeared that he would not live. We called the hospital chaplain, and he verified the baptism from the records. We were encouraged.

We consulted an attorney and asked him to represent us in the adoption procedure. We felt it might not be smooth, since we "were emotionally involved." After asking us whether we fully realized the consequences of the unusual step we were taking, he cheerfully accepted the case.

In mid-November we were summoned to court, and in a matter of minutes signed the papers that made us Todd's legal parents. There was no drama or contest, merely a brief interview with the judge.

One of the first things we did as his new parents was to take him to Cleveland Clinic for an I.Q. test. It was given by a woman who was noted for her testing of handicapped children. The results were as we had predicted. Todd's I.Q. was normal. We locked this important report in our files along with Todd's birth certificate.

The winter months passed swiftly. Todd reached his eighth birthday March 9. He was now eligible for a home tutor. I notified the school board, and Jane E. was assigned to him. She set about enthusiastically developing a communication system with Todd. He was a real challenge to teach, but Jane was equal to it. An entire new world was opening to Todd.

In late fall, a school psychologist was sent to test him. I was apprehensive, but was assured that Jane could be present to interpret for Todd, and that the test was geared to his physical handicaps.

We were greatly relieved when he finished. "He did well," the psychologist said. "My report to the state will tell them that this child will profit greatly from school."

Two weeks later, he appeared at our door again. It was apparent something serious was wrong. "I'm sorry to have to tell you," he said, "Todd does not qualify for school. I made a mistake on my test. It was brought to my attention at the office."

Anger was building furiously within me. I went to my desk and pulled from the files the report from the Cleveland Clinic. "Look at this," I demanded, thrusting the papers into his hands. "There is proof that Todd is mentally normal. Let me make this clear, too. You are now dealing with Todd's mother. If you don't give him a teacher, I will take it to court. I will put you and the county and the system that is denying this boy an education in every newspaper in this state!"

I was shaking with rage, and the poor young man was speechless.

What he reported to his superiors, I will never know, but he must have told them enough to make them reconsider. We never heard from them again. Todd's schooling was never interrupted.

Todd's intelligence was established, but his slow physical progress had been bothering me for months. He had been going to therapy for seven years now and there was little improvement in his attempts at walking. He could not control his legs and arms at the same time.

It seemed clear to me that Todd would never walk, and I began to question the value of his braces. All they did was keep him sitting straight as a soldier. Was it worthwhile encasing him in steel which prevented him from rolling about on the floor and perhaps learning to do things with his hands?

One day as I sat beside him on the floor, I told him my feelings.

"You're the one who knows how it feels to have cerebral palsy. I don't. What do you think about hanging up the braces for a while?"

He looked at me intently, thinking maybe for the first time about the possibility.

"Maybe you could learn to dress yourself, and maybe you could take care of your toilet needs. You know the braces are so heavy I won't be able to lift you on the toilet much longer."

His eyes flashed with the excitement of a challenge. He was ready to begin.

"Tonight," I said, "we'll start. You're to try to undress yourself and maybe even put on your own pajamas. Just remember one thing. Relax. Make yourself feel like an old rag doll. Then I think you'll have some control over your hands."

He was ecstatic. That evening I tossed his pajamas on the living room floor and took off his braces. "There you are. Now see if you can figure out how to undress yourself and put on those pajamas."

I left him. Soon Helenmarie popped into the room, scolding me. "Mom, have a heart! He's rubbing his elbows raw on the carpeting trying to undress."

She'll never know how guilty I felt. But I knew that Todd would keep on trying for a good long time before he threw in the towel.

An hour elapsed. I looked in on him. By this time, the rest of the children were standing around wanting to help, but he shook off their attempts. He would succeed.

Two hours went by. Todd was soaked in perspiration, but he had undressed himself and put on his pajamas. He was triumphant.

Gradually, he speeded up the process. It was amazing. If I was in another room, I could hear him sighing, drawing in deep breaths so he could relax. From that day on, except for putting on his high-laced shoes, Todd dressed and undressed himself.

In his studies, Todd continued to make progress. But there were times when I am sure his teacher wished that he could speak. He read well, especially the sports pages of the daily paper. He could be tested with multiple-choice examinations in which a nod of his head would indicate his answer.

He was in third grade when we toyed with the idea of getting him a typewriter. It would have to be an electric one, which needed only a light touch.

Bill had his doubts. "An uncontrolled thrust of his hand could wreck the thing."

But Bill had his secret hopes for Todd. One day he visited an office equipment store and explained Todd's condition. The clerk summoned a service man. Among the three of them, they came up with the idea to make a plate over the keys, with finger holes. Todd would learn to get his finger into the correct hole.

Bill built a desk in Todd's room, complete with overhead shelves to hold his books, papers, and such boyish treasures as autographed baseballs. The typewriter would be bolted to the desk.

Todd was so excited that he was more spastic than usual. "Relax. Remember, you're an old rag doll," I crooned, trying to quiet him.

I studied the situation. It was apparent that Todd couldn't concentrate on using one finger of one hand, and at the same time hold the other hand still. He was left-handed, so I tied his right hand to his wheelchair.

Next were the fingers. When he tried to use the index finger, the other four spread out and got in the way. This was solved with an old kid glove. I cut out the index finger, put his hand in it, and bound the other curled-up fingers.

Then I sat down for one of our talks.

"Todd, I've said it a million times. I don't know what it feels like to be spastic, and besides, I don't know a thing about typing. Only you know how it feels, so you are going to have to figure this out all by yourself.

"But before you try, take a deep breath and relax. Feel like an old rag doll."

With that I left him.

Bill was aghast when he heard what I had done. "He'll wreck the machine," he groaned.

As the minutes passed, doubts began to creep up on me too. Had I expected too much?

Then suddenly we heard Todd's laughter. We dashed in. He was beaming with pride and dripping with sweat.

Across the top of the page, neatly typed, was *Todd Christopher Gauchat*.

Todd grew more independent each day. He taught himself to get in and out of his wheelchair, and in and out of bed. School and sports were his joy, and his days were full with books, typewriter, and television.

Bill devised a "talking board" with the alphabet painted on it in the same order as the keys of the typewriter. With this, Todd could hold conversations with all of us, spelling out the words. This took a painfully long time, but we learned to abbreviate words, or to catch his thoughts before he completed sentences.

Todd was pure joy for me. It was exciting to watch his progress and determination. He wanted to complete his independence by learning how to feed himself, but his attempts landed in his lap or on the floor.

At this point, we turned to professional help. We enrolled Todd in Rose May Center, a residential facility for handicapped children in Cleveland. With their skilled staff, we hoped he would be able to achieve his new ambition.

It was a new experience for Todd, being away from home for the first time. But it was an enriching time of meeting new friends and adjusting to all kinds of unfamiliar situations.

After six months of intensive training, the therapists agreed that Todd would never be able to feed himself, or have a normal speech pattern. I can't say we were surprised by this prognosis; he had already achieved far more than any professional had expected.

Our family was growing and moving on too. Anita was now married. Helenmarie, a college graduate, was with the Peace Corps in El Salvador, Central America. Sue was away in college, and Eric in high school. David was still involved with his gardening, painting, caring for his menagerie, and doing as little studying as he could get away with. The state school had taken Robin from us.

Colette's problems had been diagnosed as epilepsy. But new medication had been followed by alarming new symptoms, and finally a complete mental breakdown. She was convalescing now, but years of her temporary improvements and shocking relapses had numbed our capacity for hope in her case.

Presently we had little Sue, a mongoloid child, who as an infant had always reminded me of a pink rosebud, which slowly unfolded its petals. From being the quiet one, she had turned into the mischievous one, searching out ways to tease the older children. Red-headed Joey, who had come to us at five months, was a mischief-maker, too. He was fond of rounding up shoes, blankets, toys, towels and (yes!) tooth brushes, and throwing them down the clothes chute.

Curly-haired blonde Mary joined the family when she was three.

She had pixielike eyes which made one feel she was always looking into a "never-never land."

Silvery-haired Steven was brought to us at age two. Doctors predicted that he would be a bed patient for the rest of his life. He had many problems, besides being retarded: the major one was near blindness. But he surprised everyone by learning to feed himself after years of painstaking effort; to walk haltingly (like a wound-up toy soldier); and finally to master the toilet.

Finally, there was Tiny Tim. Had he not been blind and deaf, nothing would have kept him in one place. He was a happy, energetic boy.

All these children continued to fill the house with laughter and excitement. But now Bill and I were excited ourselves about something else. We were going to celebrate our wedding anniversary, and Anita and her husband Dick had bought us round-trip tickets to El Salvador to visit Helenmarie. They even volunteered to move in and take care of the children while we were gone.

The weeks before our departure were thrilling. Travel arrangements had to be made: passports, immunizations, wardrobe. Bill had always wanted to visit the Basilica of Our Lady of Guadalupe, so we planned to stop in Mexico City on the way home.

Time went swiftly. Our departure was one week off. Bill had arranged his vacation to allow a few days off prior to departure to get rested and packed.

The last day of work, he arrived home exhausted. His color was ashen. "I think you should see the doctor before we leave," I suggested. The next day he did so.

I was outdoors with the children, who were scampering about in the dry leaves, when Bill returned. It was a golden fall day.

"Well, did you get a tonic?" I asked.

"No, the doctor wants to have X-rays and blood work done tomorrow at the hospital," he answered.

"Hey, this sounds serious."

"Probably nothing that sun and rest won't cure," he replied.

I was packing and repacking suitcases, when Bill returned from his examinations.

"Well, what's the diagnosis?" I asked almost cheerfully. Bill was silent. I looked up from my work and met his eyes. "He wants to see you. He says I have something in my lungs, and the blood tests indicated tumors somewhere in my body," he said.

I dropped into the nearest chair, unbelieving. Bill continued, "He wanted to put me in the hospital immediately."

The house was unusually quiet that evening; the bustling preparations were set aside for the moment. The stillness was broken by the ring of the telephone. A doctor in the Peace Corps headquarters in Washington was speaking. "We are sorry to tell you that we have received word from our office in El Salvador that your daughter Helenmarie has been hospitalized with hepatitis."

The voice continued, "We do not want you to be alarmed, but it can be serious, and we wanted you to know that she is being given the best care possible. We will keep you informed."

What was God trying to do to us? Two such dreadful announcements in one day. We were frantic with concern for Helenmarie, away in a strange country.

"One thing is sure," Bill said emphatically, "we are going on with what we planned. We've got to see her."

The next day I kept my appointment with the doctor. "I believe your husband has multiple myeloma," he said gently.

"What is that?"

"It is cancer of the bone."

Then he inquired, "How important is this vacation to you? I would like Bill to go into the hospital immediately."

Somehow I got the next words out. "How long does he have?"

"No one can be sure, but I would say from three to six months," he replied.

I was shocked, confused, adding and subtracting months. If the doctor was right, Helenmarie might never see her father again; she had a year remaining in the Peace Corps.

Finally, I said, "If he is as sick as you say, and has only a short time to live, I can't see that postponing the trip will make any difference. To me it's more important that he see our daughter, who is seriously ill herself."

He agreed, and gave me prescriptions for medicine which would help Bill during the trip.

How can I describe my feelings? With one stroke of God's hand, our entire life, past and future, seemed to disintegrate.

I took a roundabout way home. I found myself feeling guilty. Bill had been so tired!

Surely the foster children would have to leave now. And what of our children who were still home with us? What of Colette and Todd?

I was overwhelmed. Tears streamed down my face.

"We've got to take our lives a day at a time," I told myself at last. "We've got to remain calm and put on a strong front for the children's sake. Above all, we must pray; God will see us through."

By the time I got home, I felt a bit more at peace.

That evening, Bill and I agreed that we would put this nightmare out of our minds, and for the next two weeks enjoy every precious moment we had together.

We did just that. The beauty of El Salvador, the warmth and hospitality of Helenmarie's Peace Corps friends, and of course our time with Helenmarie, made the vacation go swiftly. Helenmarie's recovery had proceeded well, much to our relief, but it was difficult to hold back the tears as we waved goodbye to her.

Bill had seemed to weather the visit rather well, but I could sense that he was anxious to be home. We still had a stopover in Mexico to visit the Basilica of Guadalupe.

What a strange experience! Our guide awaited us in the lobby. He spoke fluent English, but he never stopped talking. We were barely on our way when he began telling us that we were wasting our time visiting the Basilica.

"Just a lot of superstitious people go there," he said. "The Basilica isn't the most beautiful one in Mexico City. Let me take you on a tour of the ancient ruins, pyramids, and museums."

There was little doubt that he was an atheist. We were polite but firm. He was downright sullen when we drove into the great square before the Basilica.

The square was crowded with school children, all lined up with their teachers supervising them. Our guide parked the car, told us to wait, and walked to the Basilica.

"Aha!" he exclaimed gleefully as he returned. "Visitors are not permitted in the church today because special services are being held for school children."

"How long?" I asked.

"It will be late this afternoon," he replied. He suggested that we tour the pyramids. On our return, we could stop at the Basilica.

Somehow the ruins did not excite us. It was tiring for Bill to walk through them. We had lunch and then instructed our guide to return us to the city. He protested, arguing that we must visit a new museum, but we insisted.

As we neared the city I could see the dome of the Basilica in the distance. At last we would see this holy place. But as we motored through the crowded streets, I realized suddenly that we were passing the Basilica.

"Stop," I cried. "We're passing Guadalupe."

"Madame," he replied, "it is late. We should be back at the hotel. Your time is up."

I answered as patiently as possible. "We hired you to take us to Gaudalupe and you promised to return. Now take us there."

He turned the car and headed for the square, which now was overflowing with pilgrims. Some were poor, others rich. Some were foreign, some native. Some carried gifts or infants in their arms; some came on crutches or in wheelchairs; some moved on their knees, saying their beads.

It was a moving sight. We wanted to take our time to observe it, but our guide hurried us along to the door of the church. We were swept along with the rest of the pilgrims, moving down the aisle. I remember Mass was being offered; but otherwise I saw nothing in the huge church except the picture of Our Lady high above the main altar.

My eyes were fixed on that picture as we moved slowly down the center aisle. All the while, our guide was chiding us about our superstition and "paganism."

I cannot remember forming a petition to her, our guide so distracted me. But as we left by a side door, I prayed, "Give me the grace for whatever lies ahead."

We had not been in the church more than five minutes. Outside our guide hurried us to the car and to the hotel. We were disappointed and yet deeply moved by our short stay.

"Did you get a chance to say a prayer?" I asked Bill.

"Yes," he said, "I prayed for Colette."

The next day we flew back to Cleveland. The following week Bill spent in the hospital, undergoing tests and examinations. For the first time, we were fully confronted with the harsh reality of the change our lives would undergo.

We put off talking about plans for the future; but privately, Bill and I were doing a lot of thinking. I was trying to brace myself for the breaking up of our foster family, and the rearranging of my life to be mother, father, and breadwinner.

On the seventh day of Bill's hospitalization, I was visiting him when the doctor came.

After the usual hellos, he hesitated.

Finally he said, "I don't know what you did while you were in Central America. But whatever it was, I suggest you return." Bill and I looked at each other, bewildered.

The doctor finished. "All the tests and examinations are negative. You can go home, Bill. You are well."

Amnesia Made Me Remember

. . . that prayer and a loving family could soften the
pain of even the most tragic loss

By MARY N. PATTON

The accident happened on my birthday. My husband, Don, had phoned asking me to meet him in town. So I bundled my tiny daughter Sarah into her zip-front snow suit, pulled on my fur-collared coat, and headed the station wagon toward Columbus. Both Sarah and I were looking forward to the day—I because it was my birthday and Sarah because happy anticipation was her natural approach to life.

Two miles from home a dark sedan ran a stop sign. As the sound of crashing metal faded, an old man's life ended and my white station wagon, now a twisted heap, settled drunkenly against the gray limestone embankment.

A nurse came running down from Rushville, the small town we had just passed. She had heard the sickening crash and knew she was needed. As she approached the gathering crowd, a burly truck driver was carrying my baby; tears in his eyes told the nurse the infant was beyond help. Sarah Ellen Patton, age ten months, died on her mother's birthday.

Immediately the nurse turned to help me. I lay limp on the edge of the road, facedown and bloody. Later, doctors credited her fast action with saving my life.

For three days in the hospital I was unconscious. But I was not without sensation. I felt myself floating outside of time, and although I knew that death was creeping slowly over me, I was consummately happy. I had no memory of the accident, no pain, no regret at leaving loved ones behind. Heaven seemed within my reach. Beautiful music played, and happy, familiar voices called, "She's coming!"

But suddenly a warm, resonant, masculine voice broke into my dreaming. "No," he said. "It is not her time!"

Paradise suddenly turned into noxious odors and strident sounds. Reality came slowly. I saw a large, two-headed man looming over me. One of the faces was Dr. Burke, our family doctor. But the grim face on the other head was unfamiliar to me.

Then the doctor's other head moved over. He was a tall, blond, intense-looking young man whom Dr. Burke introduced as the surgeon who had sewn my head after the accident. Behind him, seated wearily on a straight-back chair, I saw our assistant pastor. I learned later that he had been in my room most of the time I was unconscious.

Dr. Burke looked stern but relieved, and he seemed to reassure me. Since I was lying on my back, not a normal position for me, I tried to shift my body. A lightning flash of pain shot through me—I could hardly breathe. After a long pause, I asked, "How's Sarah?"

"Mary, remember the time you told me," Dr. Burke began, "that if one of your children was terribly hurt you wanted God to . . ."

If he finished the sentence I didn't hear him. I knew Sarah was dead. At least my baby wouldn't suffer the pain I was just beginning to endure. I looked at my doctors and security washed slowly and quietly over me.

Then I passed out. No heavenly visions this time. I just collapsed into nothingness. Since those days in the hospital, I have no fear of death. I have been there and I know its beauty.

In the days that followed I decided to fight for my life. Four children still needed me. But grief dies slowly. Sarah was gone.

Long after the pain had passed, a sad hymn or the sight of a happy child would make me cry. If I stumbled across something of Sarah's I'd break down completely. But I would try to remember that others, the Percys, the Kennedys, the Linkletters, had survived tragedies. Could I do any less?

When the doctor released me from the hospital I wasn't able to get out of bed without help. But I knew that my Aunt Laura was at home and would give me more loving care than any nurse could provide. The hospital dispensary loaded me down with pain pills, iron tablets, and Librium. But being home with my family would do more than all of these. A nurse tucked me into a wheelchair and pushed me outside. My husband was waiting in a brand-new station wagon.

Wonderful day—I was going home! But as Don turned our new car into a driveway, a chill came over me.

"Honey," I whispered, "where are we? I don't know this place!"

Don stopped the car and turned to me, surprise and apprehension on his face. "Mary, don't you know where you are? Sure you do. Come on, everyone's waiting for us inside." He could shrug it off. He wasn't feeling the tremors inside his stomach.

I couldn't remember my own house! I knew we'd searched for a long time to find the right place. But now I couldn't remember the house we'd finally chosen!

I was still in too much pain to understand that I had amnesia. Besides, I had recognized all my friends at the hospital. If I'd only forgotten what our house looked like, that would be easy enough to reconstruct with a fast tour of the place.

By the end of March I could navigate the winding staircase and renew acquaintance with my attractive home. To my delight I found two big fireplaces with cherry mantles, each flanked by white shelves which held books and china figurines and cut-glass ware.

But my delight in rediscovery was countered by my growing apprehension about amnesia.

One evening I confidently volunteered to help Aunt Laura with dinner. "I'll set the table here in the dining room," I told her. I could see the pads for the table sticking out from behind the cherry china cabinet, and naturally the tablecloth and napkins were in the drawers. Where were the dishes?

I walked into the kitchen and panicked. A bank of shelves and drawers faced me. I had organized this kitchen when we had moved here. The pots and pans were in logical places, easy to reach when cooking. The spice rack was in its niche, the silverware and dishes hid behind their door. But which one?

"Do you think you could peel the potatoes?" Aunt Laura asked. She thought I had finished with the table and, in her hurry to cook dinner, wanted me sitting down out of her way. She waved me toward the sink.

A chuck roast was browning on top of the stove. The smell was appetizing, but my knees were shaking and a knot was tightening in my stomach. "Aunt Laura, where are the potatoes?" Aunt Laura looked at me for the first time. Slowly, uncertainly, she pulled the potatoes from under the sink and brought them to me. I dissolved into tears and crumpled into her arms.

Aunt Laura washed the potatoes. She pulled out a pan from beside the oven and the peeler from a drawer. Slowly, one day at a time, I would learn to be a housewife again.

But amnesia tore my normal calm to shreds. The drugs from the hospital were no help. I began to anticipate trouble that might not even arrive. Most things I remembered correctly. Then, unexpectedly, my mind would blank out.

One evening I heard my husband arguing with our twelve-year-old son, Mike. "Don't tell her! Let her work it out!"

Work what out? I knew Don must be talking about me. So I asked Mike what was going on.

"Dad's mad at me for telling you where the clothes chute is," he answered. "He doesn't want you to feel like you've lost everything."

Even my husband couldn't understand. I knew I hadn't lost everything; only the ability to remember many things I'd taken for granted before. Don probably felt that I would remember things if I just tried harder. But it was so much easier to relearn when there was someone to lead me.

Dr. Burke shrugged when I told him about my anxiety. "You have retrograde amnesia," he said. "It is a partial loss of memory. You'll just have to learn again."

Then he made an appointment in Columbus for an EEG, to be sure I had not suffered any permanent brain damage. Since I had to be off all drugs for twenty-four hours before this test I was not looking forward to the ordeal.

But the forty-mile drive gave me time to compose myself. I had been told what to expect at the hospital: to have a clean scalp —no hairspray—where the electrodes would be fastened. I would not feel the current sent through my brain, and I was supposed to try to sleep.

As we entered the outskirts of Columbus, the freeway cut through my old neighborhood. It ran beside the vacant lot where I had dug cliff villages and trenches for toy soldiers as a child; and where the neighborhood kids had built badminton courts when were in high school. It was just an empty lot to me today. We drove past Ohio State University, where I had spent four years. We passed the football stadium I'd known like my own living room. Like my own living room, it, too, was a lost memory.

When we pulled in to the parking lot, just a mile from my parents' house, I was not surprised that I couldn't remember the hospital. Then I found that it had been built only a few years ago. I really had never seen it before.

I was beginning to understand that amnesia is not cured the way other diseases are. Its victims must relearn what they have lost.

Our daughter Laura Ann was nine that April. "Mommy, remember that cake you made for my birthday last year?" Laura Ann asked without thinking. It must have shown on my face that I couldn't remember. "It was a great big cake, made like a little girl and about as big as I was and it had yellow curls. Never mind. . . ." She ran off to the other room and I heard her rummaging in the china cabinet drawer. She came back carrying our photograph album.

There was my eight-year-old daughter, surrounded by a gaggle of giggling, smirking girls. In front of them was a birthday cake about as big as Laura Ann, a cake-girl with curly blonde hair and a grin to match those of the children grouped around it. Here was a memory rebuilt for me.

Then Laura Ann laughed and asked, "Do you remember the duck that broke its neck?"

I'd forgotten about the duck, but as I began to concentrate on the submerged memory, it slowly came back.

We had bought ten day-old ducks that spring and Don had dammed up the spring water to make them a pond. At night they slept in the chicken coop two feet off the ground, and in the morning they would fight to be the first one out the door.

One day a duck was caught in the rush and flopped out on its head. For several days we didn't realize that he had been hurt; then we noticed that he was always looking to his left. He had broken his neck and it had healed slightly askew.

We decided to let him grow. But we had to remember to put his food where his head was facing. And the kids had to lead him around buildings that were in front of him and teach him that the stream he was looking at was not the place he was running toward.

For the first time I'd found a real memory by myself. Now all the children joined in playing our private game.

Kathy came up with, "Remember the day the hamsters got loose in your car?" I couldn't. "Don't you remember?" she badgered. "We wanted to get rid of them before we moved from Columbus." According to Kathy I had packed two adult hamsters and their six offspring into our car. Kathy realized that the animals were loose as I was driving through traffic. But I still can't remember the eight hamsters scampering around my car as I threaded my way down the street.

As memories like these started to come back to me, I began to look at my life in a new way. I became acutely aware of even the smallest thing around me. If I couldn't remember something, someplace, someone, I'd just relax and admit it. I had a new world to learn and I'd make it fun.

But more and more I could pull a memory from its lock-up in my head. One day a bakery salesman came to the door. He looked familiar but his face didn't fit with any name. He was a sandy-haired young man with blue eyes, freckles, and a happy smile, all business but friendly. His eyes seemed to be saying something to me.

"Do I know you?" I asked.

"Yes, I had this route before. Think about it." Here was a challenge to dig for a memory. I could feel that he wanted me to find it for myself.

During the days before he returned I began to pull fragments of a picture from my mind. I seemed to remember talking with him about horses. We are horse fanciers and I had been chairman of a horse-show many years before—that was an event I remembered.

When the salesman came the next time I was ready with my little bit of past. Had he told me about his horse?

His face broke into a happy grin. "That's it, but it wasn't my horse. Keep digging. See you in two days." His manner seemed abrupt, but I knew that he wanted me to have the satisfaction of working it out without his help.

I began to dig harder—then I remembered. His name was Jon, and his father's horse had been named Spotted Horse Champion of Ohio one year. We had never seen it, but I remembered Jon inviting the children to come to the fairgrounds on Sunday when they were working out. He had promised to let them ride. At last I had completed another happening by myself.

Summer was a blend of physical and mental exertion. We joined a swim club that year and I worked out almost every day. I had started the summer with a dragging left leg that would pull to the outside at every step. By September I was walking naturally.

During that summer I also retackled books, and rebuilt a memory bank of recipes. I took on my sewing machine and won the battle. (Imagine starting to barbecue a chicken and remembering only how to light the charcoal; or opening your well-used sewing machine and discovering that you couldn't even thread it!)

As summer moved into autumn, the forgotten blaze of golds and red blending into magenta and brown seemed a fitting climax for my year of surprises. I'd learned to grow with pain, accept tragedy, and always to look for beauty around me.

I still often talk silently to Sarah, but I know to Whom I am really speaking, and that my child now nestles lovingly in His arms. Grief melts away. Life begins again. Each day I pray, "Thank You for my life. I am needed here."

There are many blank spots in my memory even now. But I have the pictures in the photo album, and I can delight in the family stories. Besides, now I'm building new memories. And these memories I'll keep.

I Married a Blind Man

A short experiment helped me partly to understand what life is like for my husband

By MARY E. McKENNA

I met my husband, Peter McKenna, in a hospital. I was a nurse and he was a patient undergoing his thirty-second operation for plastic surgery. A tank shell had exploded in his face a few days before the end of the second World War. He was blind.

The usual nurse-patient relationship developed into a warm friendship after he was discharged. I was amazed at how many things a blind man could do. We went to movies and plays, sports events, restaurants, dancing.

After a few months I realized that we were getting serious about each other and frankly, it frightened me. I did not think I was big enough to get involved in a permanent relationship, but Pete dispelled my fears. His gifts of flowers, candy, and Irish blarney helped in persuading me. We both prayed that we would make the right decision, and after much soul-searching on my part, we were married.

That was twenty-five years ago. Pete has never seen me, and I wonder if I have ever really seen him. No one taught me how to live with a blind husband, and I have made many mistakes. Now that our nine children are no longer taking up all my time I have decided to study blindness, to try to understand what it does to a person, my husband in particular. How does he manage to go to his vending stand every morning at 6:30 with only a white cane in his hand and a rosary in his pocket?

I tried a naive experiment. I decided to spend twenty-four hours completely blindfolded. I borrowed a pair of goggles designed to protect against infrared rays; they blocked out all light.

* * *

Being without sight for a day helped me to understand some of the physical problems, but I could not realize the psychological problems. All along I knew that tomorrow I could see again. There were the frustrations of dressing, combing my hair and hoping it looked all right, getting the coffee so hot so that I couldn't direct the spout to the cup, fixing a bowl of cereal and not knowing where the children had left the sugar bowl.

My one big accomplishment during the first hour was to empty the dishwasher and reload it. When I was interrupted by the phone, I had a difficult time going back to what I was doing. I had dried my hands and didn't know where I had put the towel. This was my usual cleaning day so I started with our small bathroom. It was strange to be wiping a mirror and not seeing yourself in it. I had to concentrate on each simple task, and I felt a real sense of accomplishment when I finished scrubbing the floor.

Our chime clock kept me alerted every fifteen minutes. I never had paid any attention to it before, and wondered why Pete was so fond of it. I heard the mailman come, but there was no point in getting the mail until my son came home for lunch. I felt my privacy invaded as he read my letters and bills. When he asked to borrow the car because it was raining I couldn't believe it, and then I realized to what extent I had lost touch with the outside world.

I fixed a sandwich, did a little dusting, and tried in vain to sort the laundry so that my daughter and I could get at it after school. I couldn't regulate the dials. My husband didn't know that I had picked this day for my "sensitivity training," so when he called and asked if I would like to go out to dinner with the children, I was relieved. It would have been a meager meal at home.

I asked him about dialing the phone, one of the ordinary procedures I had not checked out ahead of time. He told me how to count the numbers on the dial, and I felt as though I had found an old friend. I made several long overdue calls without explaining why I had so much time for chatting. You feel a certain closeness when you know the other person can't see you, either. Now I know why some of Pete's friends are so long-winded on the phone.

All day long I was reminded how much ordinary movements and habits were changed by not seeing. I tried to turn up the thermostat. I never really had paid attention to the dial; does the arrow move or do the numbers? I "watched" the news on TV and could follow the commentator's words better without a picture, but when Pearl Bailey came on singing, that I wanted to see. Several times while walking through the house I reached out for what I thought was a familiar piece of furniture, but when I couldn't recognize where I was I got panicky. When I looked for a jacket in my closet I was lost again. The clothes all felt the same. By the middle of the afternoon time began to drag and I was feeling depressed. There were so many things I could be doing if only I could see.

My patience and humility were really being tested. I learned how to bend down and pick up things without hitting my head. I learned to walk with my elbows at right angles ahead of me to protect my face. I began counting steps each time I went up or down.

When my husband came home I was so glad to "see" him that I poured each of us a glass of wine. I spilled his as I served it, and then realized that I should have used flat-bottomed juice glasses instead of stemware. Our dinner out was hilarious for the family, but I think we were a shocking sight to other diners. I noticed a hush as we walked to our table; not many young boys come in leading a blind father who is leading a blind mother! I had a bowl of soup and a sandwich, which Pete said was a cop-out.

My ego got another blow when I had to get into the passenger's seat of the car. You really have to trust in God and your son's driving ability. At each intersection I could imagine cars coming at us. I was greatly relieved to get back home to familiar territory. I took a bath and learned that you have to hang on to the soap. I tried to get interested in television, but the canned laughter was frustrating. I left the blindfold on all night, so that when I woke up I couldn't look at my illuminated dial. I heard the trusty chime clock toll three quarters of the hour, and then had to wait fifteen minutes to find out it was 4:00 A.M. Only three more hours and I would be able to see again, thank God.

When Pete was in the army hospital he met a chaplain, Father Thomas Carroll of Boston, who did much to help the men accept their loss of sight. He had spent his life working for the rights and dignity of the blind. His book, *Blindness*, has taught me much.

Before Pete lost his sight he was a hard-working, neat, fun-loving, quick-witted boy, according to his mother. He had all these same qualities after he was blind, but society labeled him with other words: blind, handicapped, afflicted. According to Father Carroll, when a person loses his sight he also suffers 20 other losses, not one by one but all together.

1. The first loss is your old way of life. This happened before I knew Pete, but from all reports he was able to accept his new life quite soon. He has said that when he came so close to death and yet survived he knew that God must have had some purpose for his life.

2. The loss of physical wholeness. We place so much value on bodily perfection that this could destroy a man's self image. Before his plastic surgery Pete's face was very disfigured. Perhaps it was a blessing that he could not see himself in a mirror. His arms were broken, so he could not even feel the scars. The plastic surgeons had to rebuild his nose, mouth, eyebrows, and facial skin.

3. The loss of confidence in remaining senses. There is wide-spread belief in a sixth sense that automatically appears when sight is gone. But there is really no increased acuteness of hearing, feeling, smelling until the blind person himself develops an awareness of noises, sounds, smoke, fragrances, and sensitive touch. Pete is adept at using all his senses and no longer has to give constant attention to the simple operations of living. He smells the salt and pepper, he listens for traffic when he crosses the street each morning, and he has very sensitive touch when he is looking for something with his hands.

4. Loss of visual background. Subconsciously we are always seeing a background, but for a person who is completely blind there is no change in color, movement, or form. For Pete it is always dark so he is attuned to the auditory background. He also has a vivid imagination and excellent recollection.

5. Loss of light security. Most people tend to relate light to sight and darkness to blindness. Light is connected with hope, beauty, and goodness, and darkness is evil, gloom, and even death. But Pete is comfortable in his lightlessness.

6. Loss of mobility. This was one of Pete's biggest hurdles. He wanted to be independent and go places. During his rehabilitation at Avon, Connecticut, he learned the Hoover cane technique which involves swinging a long white cane from side to side and literally clearing a path ahead of you. He traveled by himself through seven years of

college; he has mastered seven different house plans and landscapes, and takes the bus into downtown Minneapolis every day. He walks briskly and has the scarred shins to prove it. Rearranged furniture, doors ajar, cluttered stairways, and toys on the floor have always been taboo at our house, but there are always low branches, snow, ice, and drivers turning corners or coming out of alleys. Pete has bent many canes on those impending dangers.

7. Loss of techniques of daily living. Eating, drinking, dressing, keeping oneself neat and clean, shaving, and many other actions are all necessary operations that have to be done systematically by the blind. "A place for everything and everything in its place" is their rule. Pete has the neatest drawers. Socks, handkerchiefs, underwear, shirts, and pajamas have gone into the same place for 25 years. His wardrobe is arranged alphabetically according to color. In keeping with current style he has developed sideburns, and has discovered his own system for measuring them with an elastic band. He gets up at 5 A.M., too early for me, so that with the help of a few preparations made by me the night before, he is able to make his own breakfast. He enjoys this hour when he is on his own in the kitchen, can organize his day, and keep up with the world by listening to the radio.

8. Loss of ease of written communication. Illiteracy has commonly been equated with ignorance, another blow to the blind person's ego. When our children were little they wanted their daddy to read to them, and he tried faking it, but they caught on. Soon he had them telling him the stories from the pictures, and he had such a good imagination that he could tell them stories that were better than those in the books. Pete reads two or three books a week on his Talking Book record player. He also listens to the daily newspaper on his talking radio. The family reads to him, too; not only newspapers and books, but his mail, his records for his vending stand, and any information he needs for the various organizations he belongs to.

9. Loss of ease of spoken communication. It is difficult to listen to a person speak when you don't see his facial expression, gestures, and mannerisms. It also is difficult following a shrug of the shoulders or a nod of the head, or expressions such as "over here" or "this big." Some blind people assume an awkward posture or head movement, but Pete seems to look at whomever he addresses.

* * *

One of Pete's pet peeves is the guessing game, "Pete, guess who this is," and another is having people ask me whether he would like another serving, drink, or whatever. I try to smile and I say, "Why don't you ask him?" He uses Braille notes for his business, but they are not practical to use for public speaking. He has held several national offices in the Blinded Veterans Association, and at one time smashed all his notes as he rapped for order.

10. Loss of current information, keeping up with the times. This could be a problem when a blind person lives alone or with other blind people, but Pete lives in a sighted world and knows more about what is going on than I do. His stand is at the Minneapolis Court House, across from the police department, so he is surrounded by activity all day.

11. Loss of visual perception of the pleasurable. This is the lack of perception of objects that formerly or normally would be pleasing: a mother's face, a favorite picture, the old homestead, or something he once owned, like a new car. I think not seeing his family really bothers Pete because he never mentions it.

12. Loss of visual perception of the beautiful. If a person was sensitive to art and beauty before he lost his sight, this could be a great loss. He would have to look for auditory beauty, birds singing, water rippling, music. He could visualize beauty from descriptions by sighted people, which sometimes can be sad. But Pete is not particularly artistic, and my enthusiastic ramblings about beautiful sunsets don't excite him.

13. Loss of recreation. For an active sportsman like Pete, giving up playing football and baseball was a sacrifice. He still enjoys them as a spectator. He seeks his recreation among sighted people. He goes fishing, camping, cross-country skiing. He has tried water skiing and ice skating, and we have ridden a tandem bicycle for over fifteen years. He enjoys dancing, eating out, playing cards, and visiting friends.

14. Loss of career, vocational goal, job opportunity. The dignity of working is important to any man's ego, and people with visual problems have to overcome a lot of prejudice and public ignorance before they can take their rightful place in the working world. Pete earned a master's degree in vocational counseling, but we still have

a file of rejections from state rehabilitation agencies all over the United States. They will not hire a blind man! The Minneapolis School Board would not hire a blind teacher 20 years ago. So we started our own business, a religious gift shop, and Pete did most of the selling and restocking for twelve years. Then he went into the vending stand.

15. Loss of financial security. It is more expensive for a blind person to live if he has to take taxis, hire readers, a housekeeper, or secretary. The financial problems of the blind have been largely neglected. Father Carroll suggests a special form of insurance through Social Security. The blinded veteran gets special compensation, but financial motivation is not the only reason for a man to work. Blinded veterans could vegetate at home, but the majority are rehabilitated and employed. It decreases their dependence upon their family when they can afford to buy services, and it gives them dignity and security.

16. Loss of personal independence. We all have a need for independence and freedom. When a person loses his sight he must realize that a certain degree of dependence is forced upon him, and if he is truly mature he will accept what is necessary. Many times family, friends, or relatives try to increase their dependence.

Pete has difficulty accepting dependence, especially having to depend upon his wife. It seems to go against his Boston background.

It is difficult for me as a wife, too, to keep a balance in my role as decision maker in shopping, decorating, keeping track of the money, and disciplining the children. There are many times when his opinion could be valuable in making a decision, but through habit I often neglect to consult him first. For twenty-five years I have been in the driver's seat of our car, and this tends to make me quite independent. Sometimes I think Pete feels that it is easier to join me than fight me!

17. Loss of social adequacy. This aspect of blindness is forced upon the blind by sighted people who treat them like a minority group; not with hatred, but with pity. They have stereotyped notions of tin cups, piano tuning, and chair caning as the only possibilities for the blind. They give him free bus tickets and fishing licenses that set him apart. Pete feels he can carry his own weight financially, socially, spiritually, and every other way. He feels strongly that all

blind people should be given the opportunity to do so if they want to. People don't realize that he can rake a lawn, put a diaper on a baby, be a delegate at a political convention, or even be a pallbearer or best man.

18. Loss of privacy. He is sure to be noticed wherever he goes. Pete never wore dark glasses for the first twenty years because they seemed a symbol. Then a fellow blinded veteran whose face was more disfigured than Pete's convinced him he should wear them for cosmetic reasons. I think people should know that he is blind. When they see him in action it could change their attitudes.

19. Loss of self-esteem. The lost self-esteem has to be rebuilt right away. Fortunately that was done for Pete while he was still in the hospital. His family traveled hundreds of miles every week to visit him, and he had tremendous faith in God and his fellow man. He found unknown strength, and his Irish wit has helped him surmount almost every obstacle to rehabilitation.

20. Loss of total personality organization. Blindness involves a series of blows that can result in neurotic response. His personality, strength, philosophy, and goals make a difference in how these blows affect him. Some people never really accept their blindness except as an inconvenience, which can be dangerous both emotionally and physically.

I think our family takes Pete's blindness for granted, probably more than we should. Many times the children's friends play at our house for weeks before they realize that Dad can't see. Our own children accept it so casually that their attitude is infectious. We never tell anyone beforehand that Pete is blind, because it makes the introduction awkward and the conversation stilted.

Besides the twenty losses that occur when a person is blinded, there may be some gains. For men blinded in service, there are special educational and vocational advantages. If Pete had returned from the war in good health he probably would have gone back to his job of selling men's clothing instead of going on to college, as he did. He has had a chance to see how much goodness there is in the world. He has discovered strengths he did not know he had, and he was forced to establish a new sense of values.

He has gained many friendships, and as Father Carroll said, "Many blinded servicemen met wonderful girls, who have since become their wives, whom they would never have met if their blindness had not brought them to a particular hospital." He has been blessed with nine healthy children who love him and are proud of him. I think he holds the world's record for the number of show-and-tell programs at which he has explained Braille.

And now that I have a very small idea of what he goes through every day, I have more admiration for him than ever. It baffles me the way he can locate some twenty brands of cigarettes, hundreds of kinds of candy, and dozens of soft drinks and sandwiches at his vending stand.

Father Carroll said, "We must analyze blindness objectively and analytically before we can attempt to make the blinded person feel the subjective warmth of our love." This I have tried to do, and so on our silver wedding anniversary I say to Pete, "Grow old along with me, the best is yet to be."

A Song Is More Beautiful with Silent Harmony

My friendship with a deaf family has given my life a whole new direction

By PATSY NAUGLE

I remember distinctly the day I wrote that letter. On an impulse, I scrawled my feelings on an issue very close to me: sign language interpreting for deaf audiences. In particular, I was thinking of the audience for the 1977 inauguration of President Jimmy Carter.

I had just had a disappointing conversation with some deaf friends. I had been reading in the newspapers about Jimmy Carter's plan for his Inauguration Day, and I asked them what they thought about it. They shrugged. To them a politician was a face on a screen, with moving lips that could not be understood. They might be the president's lips, but they still meant nothing.

A few hours later, my letter was on its way to the Inaugural Committee in Washington, D.C. If Carter wanted to include everybody, I wrote, he should use interpreters, and I offered my own services.

Less than three weeks later, I received a phone call from the Committee. They planned to use interpreters in a special section for the deaf on Pennsylvania Avenue—and they would be happy to use me!

When I left San Diego for Washington, D.C., the temperature was 80 degrees. When I arrived in Washington, it was 2 degrees. I was a little worried; gloves get in the way of sign language. But it turned out that the Committee had provided a heated booth for the interpreters. It was a special thrill when President Carter and his family passed the booth on the famous inaugural walk.

While I was in Washington, I also took the opportunity to visit the chairman of the House Subcommittee on Communications. I asked him to do what he could to encourage the media to assist the deaf, and particularly to persuade the San Diego TV stations to use an interpreter on their news shows.

This invitation to the Inauguration was like the climax to a journey I had begun only two years before.

I suppose you could say I grew up on a stage. I spent most of my time performing, and my greatest goal in life was a career in drama and music. The goal was a narrow, selfish one, I found out later. Although I hadn't realized it, God had a better plan for my life, something I could never have dreamed up alone.

When I was sixteen years old, I met the Lugo family. Mr. and Mrs. Orlando Lugo and their five children were all deaf, although inherited deafness is rare. But we seemed to hit it off from the start, and before long I began to think of them as my second family. At first, we communicated by writing back and forth on pieces of paper. In addition, my sister Theresa knew sign from college, and she often interpreted for me. But I soon found that to be a true friend, I needed to speak their language myself.

There was a particular frustration involved for me here, because my life had been centered around performing, especially singing. It hurt me, each time I sang, to know that these people I loved would never hear a note. And it showed me that I had to base my life on something more than music.

The turning point was St. Valentine's Day, 1975. I decided to make a cake for my new pals, to show them how much I really loved them. I spent a long time making it, and expected my sister to accompany me, and interpret my message. But when the time came, Theresa never showed up. For the first time, I approached their house without any means of translation. I rang the bell again and again—they couldn't hear it. Nearly in tears, I could figure no way to get their attention.

Finally, they saw me through the window, and came to the door. There we stood, unable to understand each other. Yet we read the feelings in each other's eyes. We embraced each other and this silent form of communication was all we needed. But from that point on, I worked hard to learn sign.

That fall, I entered the Miss Teenage San Diego Pageant. For the talent portion of the competition, I sang, but as I sang, I translated the lyrics in sign language. I won the pageant, and I've been singing that way ever since.

During my years of friendship with the Lugos, I learned that the deaf are often misunderstood. I had always imagined that the only loss a deaf person suffered would be one of hearing, but that's only the beginning.

One of the biggest difficulties is loneliness. In school, a deaf student can be seated in the middle of a roomful of classmates, and still feel completely alone. Because they have never heard how words are pronounced, it is extremely difficult for them to speak.

Many people wonder why the deaf students cannot simply read lips. But lip reading is very difficult. To become proficient requires extensive, expensive training.

Before I became fluent in sign, I felt these same frustrations myself. In a social situation, among many deaf people using sign, I often felt left out.

I was really in love with the Lugo family. The three boys, eighteen, seventeen, and fifteen, loved to do pantomimes of all their adventures. Because sign language relies a lot on the ability to express emotions facially, the three of them are natural actors, and love to ham it up in front of their friends.

They are all athletically inclined, and all through junior high school, were valuable members of all their school's teams. As the boys reached high school, however, their athletic careers came to a heartbreaking halt. The teams there were intent on winning at any cost, and on eliminating anything which might slow them down. The Lugo boys were declared ineligible. If they wanted to seriously pursue sports, they would have to go to a boarding school exclusively for the deaf.

I felt sad to watch them go, remembering how proud their junior high had been of them. Two years before, I had watched the eldest boy walk on stage to receive an award he had worked three years to earn, an award given to only one boy in the graduating ninth-grade class. The audience had clapped loud and long, and I knew he could feel the applause in his heart.

Though deaf people everywhere face isolation most of their lives, there is one institution I know of which is helping to break down the barrier:

the Catholic Church. St. Catherine's Church, where the Lugos attend Mass with my family each week, has recently begun to incorporate deaf parishioners into the weekly services. And one of our priests has taken charge of a special program for the San Diego Diocese called The Catholic Deaf Circle. Each Mass is interpreted; the front pews are roped off for the deaf.

Once a month, we also have a speical liturgy done exclusively in sign, planned by the deaf people themselves. Hearing parishioners also have been making an effort to learn sign language.

Attending interpreted Mass has helped to break down some of my friends' shyness. The two Lugo girls, thirteen and eight, have performed with me often, both on stage and television, signing as I sing.

Because they are unable to really hear their own voices, the girls had never tried to sing themselves. But when they were exposed to our church choir, which is extremely loud, they began to feel the change from one note to another. They also found that by placing their hands on my throat as I sang, they could feel the difference between high and low notes. Recently, they've been practicing singing the scale, and a few songs, following the pattern of my voice, and the vibrations of the piano. It is still difficult to find just the right pitch, but to me, each note that rises from their lips is beautiful.

I believe that God had a purpose in bringing us together. Our friendship has helped me to grow, and the people of St. Catherine's have begun to reach out to these people also. Many wonderful new relationships are developing as a result; a brand new spirit—silent, but all the more beautiful.

VIII

COURAGE
OF THE
TERMINALLY ILL
AND THEIR
LOVED ONES

This Spring,
and Maybe Another

*Since learning that I have leukemia, I live life more
lovingly than I ever have before*

By MARIAN HODGKINSON

Five months, twenty days, and six hours ago, I visited our family
doctor.

"Your tests are in," he told me. "You have a blood disorder, which
no doubt accounts for the excessive fatigue you complained about."

"Okay, I suppose I'm anemic. How about some shots of vitamins
and stuff?" I asked.

Dr. Henderson doodled on his desk blotter, as I stirred in my chair.

"It's not as simple as that. The blood disorder you have is one we
have not yet found a cure for. You have leukemia."

There was a long pause.

"Remember, there are many things that can be done for you. There
may be a cure just around the corner. Blood cancers are frightening,
of course, but not always fatal."

Another long pause while I sat motionless.

"There are medications, new ones come out almost daily, and periods of remission that can be extended for months and even years."

"But Doctor," I said, "I have a family, a husband, and three
children."

"I know. I know."

"I don't have time for good periods and bad ones. Mine's an all-
time job."

Again, that long silence.

"I know, I know," he sighed. "Now," his voice was crisp, "let's get down to what we are going to do, starting today."

He spoke of therapy, blood transfusions, and complicated medical procedures I didn't understand. I half listened, then I interrupted. "Doctor Henderson, can you tell me how much time I have?"

"Don't worry about that yet," he said, his smile bleak.

"Tell me, Doctor, I have to know."

"You will see the spring. This one and hopefully another. Give yourself time to adjust."

I drove home following the traffic without thinking, stopping for each red signal, watching the hurrying pedestrians. All with their health, I thought bitterly. Why me?

Jim, my husband, was away on business. The children had come home from school. From the kitchen came the smell of peanut butter sandwiches and the sound of apples being chomped. "Watch those braces," I said automatically. (All our kids have braces on their teeth.)

Harmless bickering. Everything was so normal. Was leukemia going to change all that? We are a close family, not outstanding, not unusual. Three children ranging in ages from eight to almost fourteen: average students, no big behavior problems, but, I thought with a lurch in my heart, far too young to cope without a mother.

Their father is a special kind of person, a thirty-five-year-old businessman, my knight in shining armor. This had been a bad year for our business, and I had watched his hair turn gray. We also had watched our budget and were going to survive.

"Will he marry again?" Of course. Someone with a healthy body, not one that is destroying itself.

"Where's my baseball mitt, Mom?"

"In the closet under the stairs, I expect. Isn't it early for baseball?"

"Spring practice'll begin soon, coach says."

Spring so soon. This spring and maybe another, Dr. Henderson had said.

So far, I had not told Jim or anyone of my trouble. There would be time for that later on. Still, I needed a confidant, a shoulder to cry on. Having an incurable disease is a lonely business.

Daily, I walked down the street to our small church. It was quiet and usually I was the only person there. I looked at the old stained glass windows, the shabby pews, the worn kneeling benches where other desolate people had knelt and whispered, "Help me, Father, help me."

Spring has come and all my senses are sharpened. There are so many things I've never noticed before. The days are brighter, the sunsets more vivid. Sounds are clearer: the stumble of young feet on the stairs; the swish of tires on Jim's homecoming car; my oldest son cracking his knuckles.

The pattern of our lives is changing, too. Jim and I are taking the time again for long intimate talks. Recently he remarked, "Spring sure agrees with you, honey. Last winter you looked sort of strung out and pale."

I want this to be a fun spring for the children, one to remember. There'll be time for trips to the beach, to the zoo, and for backyard picnics.

I have my priorities. Who cares about dusty furniture or getting the wash done exactly on time? No more saying that I can't go with the children to the park because it's my bridge day. My favorite charity can have its bazaar without me.

And through it all I've been teaching the kids to be more self-reliant, to make their own decisions, to select their own clothes, to remember their own dental appointments. The boys can cook. Our daughter knows how to run the washing machine and irons beautifully.

Oh, I have my moments, moments of rebellion, my lonely tears, my nights of darkness and terror, my envy of well people and a legion of wishes. But over all that is a feeling of accomplishment, a knowledge that my family is self-sufficient.

God has given me time to prepare them for whatever the future holds. That word "*time*" no longer haunts me. I hold each hour lovingly in my hand; I live every day more fully than I ever have in my thirty-three years.

I pray a lot. And when I see God's face, I hear his voice saying, "Hope, Hope."

The Last, Best
Days of My Life

*Knowing that I have "Lou Gehrig's disease" has taught
me to savor each moment*

By JAMES WOLFGRAM

The calf of my right leg is going now. I noticed that last night: the weakness, the difficulty in trying to flex its wasting muscle, the many pauses necessary as I climbed the stairs. The little finger of my left hand had gone into limbo only a few weeks before, and three days later so did its stubby, forty-four-year-old companion three digits away.

This last symptom caused my eyes to get moist in front of the children, but at least there were no real tears, only the glaze of frustration. I got the bad news just one month ago: amyotrophic lateral sclerosis, the "Lou Gehrig disease." It's an insidious thing that paralyzes the nervous system, and it usually strikes in the fifth or sixth decade of life.

How many years have I left? Two, possibly? Maybe a little more? No particular therapy? No cure? Only 3,000 new cases in America a year?

I remember thanking the doctor. But now I wonder why, at the moment he told me, I saw more sorrow in his eyes than I think he saw in mine. He must be a very compassionate man.

Oh, I don't doubt there was fright in my own eyes. I'm no Iron Man, like Gehrig. They probably looked as they did on that flight into Halifax years ago when the fog and turbulence caused even a stewardess to scream. Or that night in Korea on the way to the front when the tank I was driving hung over a cliff before backing free, with the help of an Act of Contrition and a very strong reverse gear.

But those were life's fleeting things, weren't they? Then thoughts of mortality didn't linger past the next airport or the next beer-drinking session.

No, this one is It, and my first thought at hearing the news was that I had better prepare to die in a dignified manner. Five younger pairs of eyes that have yet to experience such moments will be watching. So will those of two women who share my pain: the one who gave me birth, and the one who gives me strength.

This is something I had to write, if only to tell of a peace I never had imagined possible, a revelation of the beauty in having the opportunity to set my house in order. I consider it a precious gift from God.

In the past two weeks, I have found that in my credit union the debt dies automatically with the debtor. I certainly didn't think of it that way when I signed the second mortgage papers that included something called credit life insurance.

I have found that my other life insurance policy includes a waiver of premium for temporary or permanent disability. Why? Because someone I thought of only as a salesman really had my best interests at heart.

I have been given time to go over my will. I will now have time to teach my children not to jerk the line too hard when fishing for crappie. I have time to make wonderful discoveries with my family on the gravel roads beyond the interstates. And I've even been given time to wonder at the odds of medical science finding a cure for this spectral germ that so altered my life.

I may, through vanity, hide my left hand on an impending flight to the Bahamas with my wife, but my right can still produce a husband's warmth. I can still rework my novels, though more quickly than I'd wish. I can still savor au gratin potatoes, lasagne, Caesar's salad. Now, though, there's no particular rush to finish a meal, for I have found ways to savor every second I have left to live. I also have found a time to love as I've never loved before.

There is much more. Tomorrow, I'll change a bicycle wheel instead of foisting upon others what once seemed a mindless chore. The next day, I'll watch my daughters go through their contortions at the reducing parlor instead of just driving them there and then picking them up.

The next day? Who knows? Maybe I'll just contemplate my luck. For, as God is my judge—and He soon will be—I consider myself to be among the luckiest men on earth.

Move over, Lou. There's a certain rookie coming up who learned a great deal from your life.

The Doctors Give Me
20 Years—or 20 Days

Their diagnosis: an inoperable brain tumor, "assumed to be malignant"

By DAVID MORRIS

When I awakened the morning of March 2, 1976, I felt sluggish. Slowly I realized that my legs would not support my body. Each time I tried to climb out of bed or walk, I fell. My left side was partially paralyzed; my vision was tripled.

I thought more rest would help. But after fumbling through a shower and stumbling back to bed for another hour of sleep, I was no better.

Bewildered, I clumsily dialed the telephone to talk to my doctor. After explaining my symptoms, I was told to meet him at St. Anthony's Hospital that afternoon. My parents drove me there.

I had seen the doctor only a couple of weeks earlier for a routine checkup and I felt certain my health was quite good. Now, though I felt no pain, I was frightened.

The doctor examined me, and recommended I be admitted to the hospital for further testing and evaluation. The following days didn't provide much information. The tests extended into a second week and included brain scans, EEGs, EKGs, spinal taps, neurological exams, and arterioangiograms. With each passing day, my condition worsened.

My stilted gait had become a shuffle as I continued to lose control of my legs. Physical therapy began in an effort to stem the weakening paralysis. Doug McDonald, another patient, laughingly referred to my awkward efforts to walk as "skating." At one point, while trying to run with the doctor, I fell twice.

My outlook was still optimistic, though. After all, the tests weren't showing any abnormalities, and my mental functions were intact. But I found my greatest solace in prayer. I knew that in some way all of this served a divine purpose which I could not understand. So, as I prayed, I asked for the gift of increased faith and the assurance of God's promises to His faithful.

The final test would be the CAT (Computerized Axial Tomography) scan. It was perhaps the easiest test of all. I merely lay on a table with my head in a cuplike device which fed X-ray information into a computer for analysis.

Suddenly, my doctor and the nurses seemed unwilling to discuss even ordinary topics. The next day, I was told that there was an error in the CAT scan and another would be run immediately. After the second test I was told the diagnosis: a probable brain tumor, or at best a clot. Prognosis unknown.

By now I could no longer walk under my own power. I could barely feed or dress myself. I had begun physical therapy, but that had slowly become impossible to perform.

After three weeks, the doctor sent me home. Only time would reveal whether my paralysis was caused by a tumor or a clot. A clot would slowly dissolve and loosen my knotted limbs. But what about a tumor? I prayed that the problem was the lesser of the two evils, and all would be well soon.

Once at home I created problems for everyone. I had become totally unable to care for myself. At one point, I fell down the basement stairs, hitting my head on a concrete planter. When I regained consciousness, I had not only a huge bump on my head, but my right side was getting numb.

Determined to create no additional burden upon my family, I called my doctor in the hope of returning to the hospital. He told me to come to his office for an examination.

Flanked by my father and brother, I made it to a chair in the waiting room. In the examination room, I required help to undress and get up on a table. Closing one eye, I saw my reflection in a mirror and realized how distorted my face had become.

I was told there was little doubt now that I had a tumor. The next day, I was readmitted to St. Anthony's Hospital, where another CAT scan confirmed the doctor's diagnosis: an inoperable brain tumor in the motor area, "assumed to be malignant by virtue of its effects." Three days later, I was transported to the University of Colorado Medical Center where it was felt my condition could be more adequately treated.

I was distressed to leave St. Anthony's because I had confidence in my doctor and the staff. Further, as a Catholic, I was anxious about receiving the spiritual care for which I hungered.

Upon my arrival, I waded through the mire of paper work, feeling self-conscious about my inability to speak clearly or control my hand and arm enough to sign my name. My sight had all but vanished.

As my wheelchair was gliding through the corridors, I wondered if I would ever walk out.

After a night's rest, the examinations resumed. By this time my entire left side was numb, as countless pin pricks, feather tickles, and reflex tests verified. The right side felt partially numb, and the limbs were poorly controlled.

Most of the exams were relatively painless. The pneumoencephalogram proved to be the exception, however. Imagine yourself strapped rigidly from head to foot into a small bar-stool-type seat, unable to even shift your weight, for five hours! During this time spinal fluid is withdrawn and air bubbles are injected, and a series of X-rays is taken in order to define the tumorous area.

Semiconscious, I recall being wheeled from the testing room and hearing a woman attendant call out, "This one is alive now, but I doubt he'll make it to morning." I resolved to prove her wrong.

Although not aware of it, I was taken to the intensive care unit. As I slowly regained awareness, I could hear the "beep, beep, beep" of the heart monitor. While I tried to recognize the unfamiliar surroundings, I saw two orderlies and members of my family. The strain on their faces eased as I awakened.

It seemed as though I had met death, and tasted the reality of eternity. I was amazed at the ease with which one can die. But I felt no fear, only peace and harmony.

After a few hours, I was returned to my room. My spirits were high, and I looked forward to my meeting with the doctors that evening.

Drs. Wolff Kirsch and Richard Simon entered my room silently. In somber tones, Dr. Kirsch spoke the words: "You have a few days, maybe a few weeks."

When asked about the possibility for remission or cure, he said, "Less than one percent." Then he added, "You'll fight it for a while, because you're young and strong. But in the end, you'll succumb."

* * *

Later that evening, I prayed, asking for understanding and acceptance of whatever was to come, vowing to submit to the will of God. As Easter was approaching, I couldn't help but contemplate Christ's passion, crucifixion, and resurrection, and his call to "pick up your cross and follow Me." So I passed the long night in meditation and prayer, without fear.

Reasonable hope was held out for radiation and chemotherapy. Thus began yet another stage in the battle for life. After three more arterio-angiograms, the neurological team felt certain of the dimensions of the brain growth—roughly the size of an orange. There was no obvious bulging or protrusion of the tumor.

At first I found the radiation treatments more like lying under a sun lamp than being treated for an illness. After a few days, however, the treatments made me sick to my stomach, and seemed to drain every ounce of energy. As time passed, my only response following a treatment was to sleep for an hour or two. By now Dr. Simon estimated my chances of survival had increased to 10 percent.

Next came the chemotherapy. There was an experimental drug that had been effective for others in similar circumstances. After conferring with Dr. Kirsch, I decided to try it. The medication was highly poisonous. It would attack cancerous tissue, but it could also cause kidney damage, blood deterioration, bone marrow damage. The first time I received the "chemo" was after three weeks of radiation therapy. After half an hour, I felt more nausea than I ever dreamed possible, and extreme vertigo.

After thirty-six hours, the reaction subsided. I was still numb and weak, but I had survived. I wanted to sleep.

Each day seemed to leave me weaker. The cumulative effects of radiation and chemotherapy, and the lack of physical activity, began to take their toll.

The Friday preceding Holy Week seemed to bring everything to a head. Physically drained, I couldn't crawl on all fours or stomach to the bathroom (about fifteen feet) and I was unable to hold a cup to drink. I felt as if my plug had been pulled. Amid tears I asked my family and friends to go home: "Pray for me, and be happy for me." I felt the end was coming.

Yet, I awakened in the morning. I was still weak and unable to move, but I knew that this was *not* my time.

The next Wednesday, my hair began to fall out. After three days, little remained, so my head was shaved. Now I was bald, had a patch over the right eye (to arrest multiple vision), still couldn't walk, and my speech was slurred.

Then, early one morning I awakened to see a glorious sunrise. Viewing the brilliant colors, I wondered how many priceless gifts of beauty I had taken for granted, and I resolved again to put my trust in God.

My condition slowly began to improve. Once again I had begun a routine of physical therapy, and now found moderate success. As limbs strengthened, I learned that by leaning on a wall with my hands, I could shuffle and sidestep around the edges of my room. Then I found I could hold on to a wheelchair. By pushing it in front of me, I could take slow, awkward steps. Next came a walker.

Gradually, my endurance increased. By this time, the paralysis was gone from the right side; on the left, however, only small sensations could be felt.

On Easter Sunday, 1976, my son Joey brought me a basket filled with candy and eggs. As he cautiously approached the side of my bed, I knew the worst was over. I would see his impish smile and hear his laughter again. As my wife held my hand, tears came to my eyes as I silently gave thanks for the love I knew that day.

On May 6, 1976, I was released from the Medical Center. I still required the walker, an eye patch, and the patience of those around me. Prognosis? Unknown—very poor. I might live for twenty years or twenty days.

But I am able to see, walk, write without assistance. The tumor has diminished to roughly the size of a peanut. And each day has become a bonus to me, a new opportunity to laugh, cry, and appreciate, to taste the sweetness which the Lord provides. They are free gifts, from the Head of my family.

Father Daly's Cancer

*He has gone through the same anger, resentment, and
crises of faith that other cancer victims know*

By HENRY A. KRIEGEL

Father G. Matthew Daly learned he had cancer of the colon and liver
in May, 1981. The fifty-two-year-old pastor of St. Patrick's Church
in Erie, Pennsylvania, won't talk about his illness to gain sympathy but
he is willing to share his experience to help others whose lives are
shattered by cancer.

He speaks of doctors and nurses, family and friends, the need for
faith, and the importance of a positive outlook on life.

"You can't dwell on what is really happening. You have to learn
to go about your business to the best of your ability. If you can't develop
a positive attitude, you won't survive it. People who are positive about
what they're doing have fooled the doctors by living years beyond the
predicted two or three weeks."

Like most cancer patients, Father Daly recalls complaining of tiredness
almost a year before the malignancy was diagnosed. He says he was
tired and achy and couldn't wait to get to bed at night. He was hospitalized in May, 1981, for apparent hepatitis when doctors discovered
the colon cancer which had already spread to the liver.

"You don't want to believe what you're hearing, and doctors are
reluctant to use the word '*cancer*.' They want to send you on for further
examinations. I went through depression when I first realized what had
happened. The same was true with my close friends—we shared that
depression completely."

Father Daly recalls how he pressured the doctors to tell him how
long he had to live. "I was hearing anything from three weeks to nobody

really knows, and it is devastating. And when that's over with, you get angry and start asking, 'Why me?' You get very angry at yourself— not necessarily at God. Even though He becomes a victim of your anger, you wonder if you did something to cause it, if it can really be true, and so on.

"Another reaction is resentment—and I was surprised at that one —resenting other people who are well."

When he was out of the hospital between surgeries he would ride down the street seeing kids on bikes, old people walking in the park. "I resented their freedom and their health. It took a while to put the pieces together on that.

"It isn't just one complete set of emotions and it's over with. These things come back periodically. The last time I was at the clinic and was told the treatment wasn't working, all the emotions came back again." His voice trails off into a moment of silent reflection.

"Some people are so annoyed about their reaction, but they have to realize that it's normal. I've talked to so many people about this and they seem relieved to know that a priest goes through it all, too."

Father Daly says the eventual reaction you hope for is acceptance —"and it took a long while for that to surface." He adds that you don't come to acceptance alone—faith and friends are an essential part of that. He speaks of the need for family and friends being there—and perhaps not in the way we think they should be.

"In the first few days, just their being there was enough—as many as fifty priests were in and out, both bishops came to see me. Nothing reaffirmed me as much as that. If I wanted to cry, I could, and that's a great help. There isn't a lot you can say—I say far less to people in those situations now than I ever did before."

"And then, there's prayer," he says. "It was one of the first times in my life when I experienced how the prayers of so many people can lift you up. I really felt at times that I wasn't doing it all by myself."

He is still hesitant to discuss his illness. "I don't want to brag about it or gloat over the anxiety that is part of it," and his voice trails off again. "I wish I didn't even have to talk about it at all."

His reflections keep returning to faith. "It's there as you try to resolve that question, 'Why?' And you get nowhere with it. You have to ask, 'Why not? Why should we be exempt from suffering and pain?' and you can't resolve that unless you believe in God. You have to realize that there must be some purpose to your suffering. People without any faith would continue to ask 'Why?' and then they can't face it.

"I became aware of an absence of faith when I was at the clinic. So many doctors and nurses didn't have any. Even in talking to them, it was all medicine. They were self-sufficient. It was up to them whether or not I came through the surgery. One doctor even told me he hoped everything went well with my surgery and I added, 'And I hope God's with you.' And he said, 'Well, I've never seen a miracle on the operating table.' That hurt. And yet there were other doctors and nurses who obviously had a faith you could sense. They were the ones who sustained me."

In looking back over his experience, Father Daly remembers something else important to cancer patients. "One of our priests said to me, 'You've reached a point where you realize you are fully dependent upon God.' Right now all I can do is take medicine—there's nothing more I can do. And at that point you have to give yourself entirely to God and say, 'Well, here I am, everything else is up to You.'

"Many cancer patients blame themselves for having caused it and feel they should be involved in some frantic activity to get rid of it. It's nonsense to blame yourself. You have to get rid of that guilt. And the idea that you should be doing something through your own efforts is also foolish. You just bear through it, you develop a positive attitude, you listen to the doctor, but you realize that God is the final answer."

He is eager to speak to doctors and nurses about the need for empathy with patients. "They have to have the same positive attitude they want their patients to have. They can't be perfunctory with their duties. That frustrates the patient."

He shudders as he recalls a patient who was in isolation. The doctor came in one day, tore down the isolation sign, and said to the patient, "Well, you won't need this any more. We've found out the real problem. You have cancer," and left.

"Even though patients think they want to know the worst, they usually don't. And doctors have to be more cautious in what they say to patients.

"The compassion of nurses and doctors—even though they are so busy—is eighty percent of the care they give. When I'd be lying there for such long hours and a nurse would come in and just say something comforting rather than just doing her work—you don't know what a boost that was."

Father Daly is still shy about the question of his illness. And yet he's willing to share to help others. He's open and honest about the experience. And most of all, he's filled with hope.

He's also reached beyond himself to help other cancer patients through a Mass celebrated recently at St. Patrick's Church for victims of cancer and their families. "If I can do more, I will. By the grace of God, I don't want my life to be wasted."

My Last Years
with Barbara

*I can hide nothing; when I walked into her room she
knew something was wrong*

By DALE FRANCIS*

We had known something was wrong. It was in May when Barbara
first started coughing. We went to the doctor the very first week.

He diagnosed it as bronchitis. Later when it persisted and tests
showed nothing, he sent her to an allergist. Barbara had always had a
sensitivity to pollens and so he treated her. It seemed to help.

The illness was never disabling. We both thought of it as just a
bothersome allergy. During the whole time she was under the doctor's
care, she had all the tests that she could have been expected to have.

We really knew something was seriously wrong because of a photograph. We were asked to be the godparents for a baby boy born in
the parish. There were photographs taken and one of them was given
to us.

When you are with someone all of the time you are unaware of
physical changes. But when Barbara saw the photograph she was surprised. There were lines in her face she had not had before; there was
a kind of grayness in her complexion. "I look like someone who is
very seriously ill," she said. And, although I had not really been aware
of it before, I could look at the photograph and see that it was true.

She had started having a low-grade temperature, but the allergy
specialist was not greatly concerned. He had treated her since she was
a little girl, and had seen patterns in her reactions to allergies not really

*Dale Francis, for many years executive editor of *Our Sunday Visitor*, is now
executive editor of the Washington (D.C.) *Catholic Standard*.

much different from those she had now. When the coughing persisted he had X-rays taken but there was no indication of any problem.

We had little money, but I decided in midwinter that is might help if she had some sunshine. The way things always seemed to happen for us, it turned out to be possible. There was a letter in the mail from an old friend, an Episcopalian priest, Father Clarence Petrie. There were things he wanted to talk about. He wondered if we would come to Clewiston, Florida, to visit for a while. He had arranged for us to have an apartment for three weeks.

The sunshine helped. The cough subsided. Being with Father Petrie, who had spiritual problems he want to talk about, turned us both from thinking about her illness. But the last week the fever came back, now 102 degrees and more. A doctor there said he could not find the cause; he urged us to get to the hospital for a thorough checkup when we returned home.

At Mercy Hospital, Barbara was given a room but she didn't stay in bed. She visited with the Sisters, and with friends who were in the hospital; she went for her tests but not with any sense of being a patient.

I literally sweated out the results of those tests. The worry grew for me. The next day I went to the Sister who was in charge of the hospital and told her how worried I was.

She smiled. "There's really nothing to worry about," she said. "Barbara is all right. It is a good thing to get everything checked but I'm sure she's all right. We visited yesterday and she surely doesn't seem ill."

To assure me she called the laboratory. "Can you give me the report on the tests on Barbara Francis?" she asked someone. The smile vanished from her face, her voice lowered. "I see," she said. "I see."

She put the phone down; for a few seconds she sat there, looking down at her desk. Then she turned to me. "I'm sorry, Dale. It really is very serious. Charlie wants to talk with you." She meant our family doctor, Charlie Norris, who had been Barbara's classmate in grade school.

He was on the first floor in the room they had for doctors. There was pain in his face. "It's Hodgkin's disease," he said without any preliminaries.

"Hodgkin's disease?" I'd never even heard of it.

"It is a cancer of the lymph glands. I'm sorry, Dale, but it is terminal."

Charlie went on talking, telling me more of the illness, saying there could be no specific prognosis, that it might be months, that it could be years. There was really no way of knowing, except at this time there was no hope for recovery. The illness was terminal. Terminal. That word kept ringing in my head.

"Have you told Barbara?" I asked him.

"No," he said. "I thought you would want to do that. Sometimes it is best not to tell patients everything. I thought you should be the one to decide."

I knew Barbara and there really wasn't any decision that had to be made. "She will want to know," I said.

I can hide nothing; everything goes to my face. When I walked into her room she knew something was wrong. "You look like the bearer of sad tidings," she said, smiling.

So I told her. How I told her I do not know, but I told her.

The smile didn't leave her face. "I thought it was going to be serious," she said. "This Hodgkin's disease, what's that?"

So I explained. I told her there were large growths around her lungs, that the snip from a swelling in her armpit had given them the diagnosis.

"It is terminal," I said.

She laughed, "Life is terminal."

She comforted me when I had come to comfort her. "Look," she said. "We'll fight this old Hodgkin's disease. We won't give up. There's a lot of life in this old girl yet, you just wait and see."

And then she talked of the children, Guy and Marianne. "They are too young to understand. If I have to be in the hospital we'll just say mother isn't feeling well."

She was still smiling when I left. I drove home in a daze. Fannie Carr was taking care of the children and she would be waiting to get home.

Marianne was not yet three. She came running to me. "How's Mommy?" she asked.

"She said I should tell you and Guy that she loves you very much and she sends you each a kiss," I said and I hugged her hard, holding her tight.

Fannie was concerned. She had worked for Barbara's parents for many years and had known Barbara from childhood. "How is Miss Barbara?" she asked me when we were alone. "She's really pretty sick," I said, "but I think she is going to be all right." "Thank the Lord for that," Fannie said.

I gave the children their supper, said their prayers with them, and put them to bed. As I sat in the living room, a thousand thoughts rushed through my mind. Barbara was just thirty-eight. The phone rang.

It was one of the student nurses; I'd known her from the time she was a little girl. "Dale," she started out, "there's something I want to know. We've been talking about it. Does Barbara know what her illness is?"

"Yes, she knows," I said.

"I knew it," she said. "The other girls said it couldn't be true. She was out in the hall, talking and laughing with the nurses. She went down to Mrs. Beatty's room and was cheering her up. They said she couldn't know, that no one who knew could be laughing and talking. But I knew, Dale, because I know Barbara."

I sat down and, finally, tears came. Yes, she knew Barbara.

Barbara was home a few days later. They began X-ray treatment, bombarding the areas where there were tumors. Charlie had warned the X-rays might nauseate her, but almost by an act of will she didn't allow that to happen.

She started working again at the Catholic Information Center we had in downtown Charlotte. It was almost as if there were no illness at all.

She took it all so casually that it bothered me. She did everything just as she had done before. She didn't rest, she didn't even seem to be doing anything to take care of herself. One Sunday afternoon I talked to her. "Look," I said, "you've got to take this seriously. You've got to take it easy; rest so you'll keep your strength. Don't you understand you have a terminal illness?"

"All right, all right," she said. "I hereby promise I will take my terminal illness seriously."

Then she started laughing and I started laughing and we couldn't stop laughing. The doorbell rang. We opened the door. It was Art Linsky and his new wife. We'd known Art at Notre Dame and he had come to live in Charlotte, too.

"What's so funny?" he said.

"Just a private joke," I said and we laughed some more. When they had left we laughed again.

We had a dream, a far-off dream because there was no early chance of realization. We wanted one day to visit Europe, to go to Lourdes, to visit Rome, to visit Fatima in Portugal and to go to Spain and France and England.

Now there was no time for dreams in some far-off future; there weren't years ahead of us, there were only months. But I told her I had made a decision. "We're going to make that trip to Europe," I said.

"Why not the moon as a side trip?" she asked. "You do understand we have no money, don't you?"

I understood. I'd left a good position at the University of Notre Dame to come to the least Catholic city in the entire nation to open a Catholic Information Center in the heart of the city. And it was successful, but not financially. We barely had enough to put food on our table, to run our old car, to meet the house payments.

But I didn't care. If we were going to make our trip to Europe, we had to make it now.

I went down to the Carolina Motor Club. I got all the books, started planning our trip. We would go first to Fatima, then to Spain where we had friends in the Opus Dei, then to Rome and Assisi and Florence and Venice. From there we would go to Paris, to visit Notre Dame and 23 rue du Bac, where Our Lady appeared to St. Catherine Labouré. Finally we would go to London.

I came home with the itinerary all worked out and told Barbara where we would go. She laughed, "It's a wonderful trip. I'll be glad to go with you. Now let's look at the old bank account."

A man phoned on Sunday morning, soon after we'd come back from Mass. His name, he said, was George Strake. He was from Houston. He knew me from the column I wrote in *Our Sunday Visitor*. He said he would like to talk to me. He didn't have a car and wondered if we could come to the airport to see him.

He took us aboard his private plane to talk to us. It was fixed up like a living room. The children climbed over the furniture as we talked.

He explained he had heard of Barbara's illness. I do not remember if he told us how. He said he thought we should go to Europe, to Fatima, to Lourdes, to Rome, to Assisi, to Florence, to Venice, to Paris, and to London. He had arranged it all. He had the tickets, he would provide us with other money for incidentals. He wanted it to be his gift to us.

We had told no one of what we had planned. I hadn't even prayed about it. Praying for things for ourselves is something that just never occurs to me. But I had planned the trip we would take and in every detail it was the same as the one George Strake had planned for us.

When we got back home Barbara picked up the folders, looked them over. Then with her southern accent she said, "Now don't that beat all."

The trip was all that we dreamed it would be. There was almost no one at Fatima when we were there but the bareness of it all seemed just right. A young couple were being married at a little chapel in the great courtyard of the church, and we knelt with their friends and prayed for their happiness and cheered them as they walked out of the chapel. We decided Lourdes was the most beautiful place in the world.

Mr. Strake had provided for us in Rome. Some years before, he had met Monsignor Giovanni Montini and told him in passing that if there was ever some special need the monsignor should call on him. A few weeks later Monsignor Montini called on him. The Vatican wanted to begin excavations under St. Peter's in hope of finding the tomb of St. Peter. It would cost about a million dollars. George Strake, whose charities were so great that no one really knows of them all, sent the money for the excavations. It was done, as were most of the things Mr. Strake did, without any publicity.

When Mr. Strake told them friends of his were coming to Rome, there was nothing they wouldn't do for us. Monsignor Joseph McGeough, an American in the papal diplomatic corps, was our host.

He took us in his car to all the places we wanted to visit—to Netunno and the chapel of St. Maria Goretti, to the room where my favorite saint, St. Benedict Joseph Labre, had died. Monsignor Montini, who was to become Pope Paul VI, welcomed us. We talked a long time of the plans I had for a Catholic information bureau in Washington and he was enthusiastic.

Pope Pius XII was not well. He was having no audiences, but he came to his window to give the crowd in St. Peter's Square his blessing.

We visited Assisi and Florence and Venice. We were in the cathedral in Venice when Cardinal Roncalli came into the church alone. He moved from the altar to a place not far from us and we introduced ourselves and talked with him a little while, never even guessing that this heavy old man would be the next Pope, John XXIII.

We were in Milan for only a few hours but we received a strange blessing. The first church we entered was just starting Benediction, a devotion we loved. When Benediction was over we walked to another church. As we entered, Benediction was just beginning. By the most remarkable coincidence we visited five churches that afternoon and each time just as Benediction began.

"I don't remember having been Benedicted so many times in all my life," Barbara said.

Paris was wonderful. The chapel at 23 rue du Bac drew us most of all. We never saw the Louvre, and we missed all the places tourists always go. Almost all of our time was spent in the chapel where the incorrupted body of St. Catherine Labouré lies, and where the tomb of St. Vincent de Paul is. It drew us again and again and we spent most of the four days kneeling there.

London gave us lots of book stores, and Mass at the Farm Street church celebrated by Father Martin D'Arcy, a priest we had long admired for his writings.

We stayed at Claridge's; Mr. Strake had arranged everything first class. The last evening we had dinner in the dining room where an orchestra was playing and people were dancing on a ballroom floor.

Barbara was a good dancer and liked to dance, but I'd never learned, and after a few hopeless efforts to teach me she had given up.

I forget what song the orchestra was playing. I should remember things like that but I don't.

"Hey, double left foot, how about one last dance?" she said.

So we got up and we danced our last dance.

When death came in 1961, it was almost seven years to the day since Barbara had first become ill.

By then I had worked for four years in Austin, Texas. I did public relations for St. Edward's University there, and taught a few classes. And I had started a diocesan paper, with the encouragement of Bishop Louis Reicher, and the business know-how of a friend from my youth, Jim Houser.

There was a cemetery back of St. Edward's, a beautiful place alongside a busy highway. "I suppose that is where I'll be buried," Barbara had said, the day we arrived in Austin, looking at it not with sadness but interest. It was.

The years in Austin were difficult but productive for Barbara. She wrote a column for our paper; kept working on the novel Doubleday had sent her a contract for before it was finished; got involved in a dozen projects helping others. And all the time she was growing more and more ill.

A doctor in Houston, Dr. Jack Rose, was working on a new treatment for Hodgkin's disease, and he took her as a patient. There would be periods of remission, then the disease would come back more fiercely than ever.

Sometimes the pain would be unbearable. Medication caused severe hives. Once in pain Barbara tried to get out of bed at a hospital, fell, and fractured her skull. The tumors distorted her face, her neck was swollen almost to grotesqueness.

Once I came to the hospital room and she was looking at herself in the mirror. "Man, I'm a mess," she said. The last year she was in the hospital more often than she was at home.

Yet Barbara never really was a patient. When she was well enough to do it she was out in the halls, visiting other people. In Houston, where many Hodgkin's disease patients had come for treatment by Dr. Rose, they called her their cheerleader. She came to know each of the patients as friends and mourned when they died.

She never complained, but once I heard her almost complain. It was in the middle of the night. We slept in different rooms because she said I had to get my rest and I'd never get it the way she was turning and tossing.

Her voice woke me up. She was speaking earnestly, as if the one to whom she was talking was in the room with her.

"Listen," she said. "I know You never give anyone a cross heavier than they can carry. I know that all right and I believe it. But I'll tell You right now your idea of what I can bear is a whole lot more than I think I can."

In the last weeks all of the disfiguration disappeared. There was no more swelling. Her neck and face became as they were before she was ill. There was even less pain.

"What do you know," she said one day looking into a hand mirror. "I'm pretty again." And she was.

She knew the day she was dying. She explained it to me. "I don't really feel bad. It is just that my legs are so hard and so cold, like they are stone."

Benedictine Father Emeric Lawrence, one of our closest friends and the priest who witnessed our marriage, was in France, and he had written Barbara a letter about dying. Unaccountably, it had been delayed in the mail for more than two months and arrived only that day. It was a letter that was meant to help her face death and it was beautiful. I read it to her and she smiled. "Isn't that just like Father Emeric to come to help me die," she said. She had me read it over and over to her.

A great many people came by and as soon as they came she would have them join her in prayers for the dying.

She had made all her plans. She had many instructions for me. She was never pleased that I wore jeans and had to be forced to wear a tie and coat. She was stern about it. "I mean it, Dale. You have a position in life. Most of the time you dress like a bum. I want you to start dressing better."

She had other directions, too. She gave them to the Sisters. "When I die I don't want them to take my body out until there's nobody in the halls. That would just make people sad and I don't want people to be sad."

It was about seven o'clock when she said to me, "You haven't had anything to eat all day. I want you to go out and get yourself something to eat."

I said Sister would bring me something from the kitchen. She shook her head. "I want you to go out, Dale, I want you to go someplace and get yourself a hamburger and milk shake. I'll be all right. I want you to go out, Dale."

So I went. They said it was only a few minutes after I left that she hemorrhaged terribly and went into unconsciousness. I returned a half hour later and she was gone.

I went home. Josefa and Marianne were waiting for me. "She died," I said. Josefa began weeping. Marianne looked at me, unbelieving.

Guy, our brain-injured son, was asleep. I didn't tell him until morning. He tried to understand, looked puzzled and then asked, "Mommy with Jesus?"

I said, "Yes, Mommy's with Jesus."

He clapped his hands in joy, "Mommy's with Jesus, Mommy's with Jesus." Then suddenly he stopped. He looked at me, startled by the understanding. "I don't want Mommy with Jesus. I want Mommy with me. I don't want Mommy with Jesus, I want Mommy with me."

And he wept, all of us together wept. For me the weeping would not stop. Barbara had said she didn't want sadness when she died but that couldn't stop the sadness. It was Marianne who stopped my tears. I was weeping alone and she came to me.

"Daddy, should we be happy that Mommy has gone to Heaven?"

I said we should be.

"I don't think Mommy would want you to cry."

So I stopped my weeping.

The funeral Mass was on the Feast of Corpus Christi. Barbara would have wanted that. Whether it was liturgically proper or not, I don't know, but for her funeral Mass Monsignor Maurice Deason, our pastor, celebrated the Mass for the Feast of Corpus Christi. Everyone in the church, crowded to the walls, received Holy Communion. Barbara had said she wanted that.

A strange thing happened that morning just before the funeral Mass. I'd found an old brown suit in my closet. I'd had it a long time but hardly ever wore it. But I remembered what Barbara had told me about dressing right and I put it on. I was at the church when I noticed I was wearing old black shoes. I hadn't thought of that at all and didn't even have any brown shoes. But it wasn't right, wearing black shoes and a brown suit.

And suddenly there was something I knew; how, I have no idea at all. I went to the rectory and Monsignor Deason's mother answered the bell.

"Mrs. Deason," I said. "I need some brown shoes to go with my suit. You have some brown shoes that I can wear."

"I'm sorry, Dale," she said. "Father doesn't have any brown shoes at all."

"I know where they are, Mrs. Deason," I said, although I had no idea why I was saying it. "They're around in a back hallway. Near the back door."

"Well, if you know where they are just come on in and get them," she said.

They were exactly where I knew they were. They were shiny new shoes and they fit me exactly. I put them on.

So I went to Mass looking like the gentleman Barbara had told me I should. My mind was too much occupied with other things to even think about it, but when the Mass was over and Barbara's body was placed in a grave, the wonder of it struck me.

I asked Father Deason about it. For a while he couldn't think what I was talking about. Then he said, "That's strange. Just before I was going over for Mass there was a man at the back door. I didn't know who he was. He handed me the shoes, said he didn't need them anymore and somebody would be needing them. I just put them down on the floor near the door and went to the church. I hadn't even thought about it until now."

I could hear Barbara laughing. "Now don't that beat all."

IX

COURAGE
IN FACING
DEATH

Mother Wanted
Death with Dignity

She died quietly, beautifully, bathed in the love
of her children

By CORNELIA HOLBERT

January 2, 1977. 9:45 P.M. The body in hospital room 7022 was tiny. Both arms were in restraints, the I.V. connected to its bottle; nasal cannulae on a Y-shaped frame, which went under the chin and behind the head, connected to a bottle of oxygen.

Eyes were closed. When my younger brother Jim told her I was there, and I leaned down to kiss her, she slowly and carefully said, "Why must I suffer?"

(University Medical Center summary: "This eighty-six-year-old woman was admitted on Jan. 1, 1977, for a left hemiplegia [paralysis of half the body]. She has a history of cerebral arteriosclerotic vascular disease since 1966. The patient has had three episodes of transient cerebral ischemia [small strokes] over the last ten years, the most recent in June of 1976, with weakness of the right hand which cleared within two days. The patient did well until the night of Dec. 31, 1976, when, after dinner, she slumped over her chair and had a left hemiplegia. Chest X-ray showed left lobar pneumonia. Therapy was initiated with intravenous fluids and antibiotics.")

At the nurses' station, my brother and I were told courteously that the doctor would not be in until morning, nor was a resident available: "We are doing everything we can for her. *Everything.*"

Oh, God. I had come 2000 miles to respond to my mother's request of years' standing. "Don't let them keep me going if I have a stroke. Promise. Promise me."

215

11:30 P.M. The night nurse let me stay for a couple of hours, in and out. But then she assured me that Mother would rest better if I stayed away. I was angry, but as I looked in cautiously I saw that the nurse was right. Darkness and no sounds of restlessness. I stayed in the waiting room with a woman whose father was also in coma from a stroke.

January 3. 1977. 5:30 A.M. A call to my husband to tally with 6:30 in New York, when he would be preparing to go to his own hospital to see his patients. Would he confirm to the doctor here in Texas that Mother had always asked not to be kept going when the large stroke came? He would.

6:30 A.M. Jim arrived and we were able to send the nurse home. Mother was restless.

7 A.M. The doctor arrived and we presented him immediately with my husband's confirmation and our request to remove all supports. A brain scan had been ordered for that morning to determine the amount of damage, but the doctor agreed to our request to do nothing further.

A thorough clinician, he then made another complete examination, reporting that the pneumonia was more extensive and adding, of the coma, "She *is* deeper in." The only thing they would keep going, he said, was the I.V. "It's unkind to take a patient off I.V.," he explained.

We pointed out that, despite uninterrupted I.V. for forty-eight hours, her mouth was parched, her tongue like a small piece of wood, her lips cracked and peeling. We begged for water instead, as she was breathing through her mouth.

(Hospital summary: "By 1/3/77, the family insisted on no intravenous fluids and no antibiotics being given to the patient, because of the patient's own wishes, and the patient was then treated with ice water and Haldol for restlessness, and Demerol for pain.")

7:15 A.M. Restraints and I.V. were removed. Immediately, the right hand went up to try drawing out the nasal cannulae. No problem with the left hand, no resistance, no interference, but I caught my breath at the sight of it—bruised and swollen from elbow to wrist, presumably from the tourniquet for blood specimens, the I.V.—but that was ended. Now she could be turned on one side or the other, curl up or stretch out and, most important, use her right hand to communicate.

Mother slept quietly. She did not rouse when she was anointed.

10 A.M. Now her real work of that day was under way. Perhaps it could be described only by a person with severe asthma. The work of breathing.

"You can try it yourself," an asthmatic once told me. "Hold your breath as long as you can, and then, instead of taking a deep gulp of air, sip it, just taste it. And then do it over again, and again, as long as you can. That way, maybe you can tell what it's like."

I watched the small shoulders lifting and sinking, struggling endlessly, but bravely, never a complaint after last night's "Why must I suffer?" She had asked to be allowed to work this out, and she was doing it. Eyes always closed. The panting breath to a rhythm that seemed to say, *I am coming, I am coming*.

For a few hours, she could signal yes and no to questions: Shall I rub your back? Do you wish to be turned?

Water, the primal blessing. First half-spoons of ice water, but frequently they caused choking. My brother's idea was better: a facecloth dipped in water, squeezed drop-by-drop into her mouth. Parched lips were smoothed with Vaseline.

Finally, the perfect system presented itself, biblical, intimate, a sign of love: a fingertip dipped in ice water and smoothed over the tongue. No randomness now, every dry spot moistened. She tilted her head back slightly on the pillow, like a child, to receive the strokes.

Restless drowsiness, restless wakefulness. She was turned, medicated; she breathed with increasing effort and rapidity. But courage. No complaints. We communicated with words and responding pressure of the hand.

"Daddy is watching you now, helping. He is waiting for you. He has been waiting so long for you. . . ."

Noon. During the morning, a certain frosty distaste for this procedure in room 7022 had been evident among floor personnel. I could appreciate this; if one wishes to dies in peace, she should not go to a hospital, where the objective is recovery at all costs.

But by noon, the chill had lifted. In addition to those coming to the room on routine duties, other nurses and aides stopped in occasionally in a friendly way to see how things were going. One even said she was praying for us.

3 P.M. Jim's wife, Joni, arrived with a small statue of Mary she had found in Mother's things. Mother clutched it, put it to her mouth to kiss it, held it there. But the nurse was concerned for injury, so while my brother stood guard, I went to the gift shop of that huge medical center to a buy a rosary. None was available. I found a good substitute, though, in a string of small beads spaced out on a chain. Mother clasped them in her hand and allowed the statue to be placed under her pillow.

5:00 to 8:00 P.M. Restless, breathing more rapidly, responding to words, never complaining. Love and admiration at her courage had been mounting all through the day, and now, to crown my frequent declarations, I found myself giving what she knew was the accolade: "You're great. You are as great as Daddy."

Years of misunderstanding, of defense and rejection and judgment and bitterness, flooded clean. I was able to ask her forgiveness of all my sins and she to respond freely and ask mine, with the small strong hand. Love flowed now, not merely the love of compassion but the love of adoration before the glory of a soul stripped down to its essence, the God there, all the beauty not seen before by me since unremembered childhood days. Grace and love flowed over us both. I held her and we kissed, over and over.

9:00 P.M. Breathing was now so rapid that it exceeded my pulse rate. The doctor examined her and ordered additional medication for restlessness if it should be needed. He agreed that this might be the night.

January 4, 1977.1 A.M. Belatedly, it occurred to me that Mother might want me to pray aloud. Her response was a strong pressure of the hand. So I began the Rosary, her lifelong devotion, and had gone through the first two mysteries, not doubting which they should be: the Resurrection and the Ascension.

Then a new thought came: "Shall I tell you about the book I'm reading? It's *Mary*, by Sholem Asch. You'd like it. It's full of Jewish customs and laws. The fictional parts are beautifully done."

The pressure of the hand then. Not only did she love Mary, but she had been a reader all her life, and at seventy-four had even begun to review books.

For fifteen minutes, while I told her of *Mary* as far as I had read it, she lay perfectly quiet and attentive—no restlessness, breathing somewhat quieter, the mind transcending the body.

How many hours could I have lightened in this manner before, instead of the constant solicitude of "Do you want this?" and "How does that feel?" I should have thought of this sooner, because in June, when she was sick, we had read to each other constantly.

2:00 A.M. Suddenly the quality of the breathing changed. So this was it. I thanked God. She seemed to be in no discomfort, not *having* to breathe; not gasping, not moving her shoulders with effort, just sending out a sound like that of an oak leaf shaken rhythmically by tiny gusts of wind, and the sound formed words in my mind: *Hal* le *lu* jah, *Hal* le *lu* jah.

Was she seeing something that brought that glory? Was this like watching a birth, the soul trying to escape through that little mouth?

3:00 A.M. But Mother continued alert, and death did not seem so imminent. I asked if she would like me to call Jim. Yes, said the hand. When I returned from the phone she pulled lightly on the front of my dress, which I took to mean I was to kiss and hold her. No. To explain, she again touched my dress and then the neck of her hospital gown. "You want me to change your gown before Jim comes?" Yes.

Then a touch of perfume for her hair. Not that she was strong enough to reach her own hand so far, but I knew that was part of the plan. This done I could even jest: "You'll wait for Jim now, won't you? It will take him about fifteen minutes. You *will* wait?" The hand, even a smile.

3:20 A.M. Jim arrived, her beloved son, and sat with her until 7:00 A.M., talking, holding her hand.

7:00 A.M. Breathing suddenly altered. The slightly strained look left her face and it became a fine ivory mask. An hour more of the mild, intermittent sighs of that terminal breathing, and then *Free at last! Free at last!*

John, Lois, and Father George Carry Their Crosses

They all accepted their trials and inspired others with their faith

By BOB SANTOR

John Philip Downs got his B.A. at Bellarmine Franciscan College, Louisville, in 1967. He tried to enlist in the Army, but was turned down because of defective eyesight.

So he applied for field service with the Red Cross. After his orientation, and courses in the Vietnamese language, he spent a year in the South Vietnamese countryside serving GI's and anyone else in need.

It irked him when Americans and others, too narrow-minded to appreciate the country's ancient culture, called the people "gooks," or worse. One night he was awakened by a baby crying from hunger. As the oldest boy in a family of eleven children, he knew the sound. He wrote home that it struck him we are all born in the same helpless condition, and all babies cry in the same way for the same things, all over the earth, regardless of color, nationality, or culture.

"Working for this outfit changes your whole idea of being a part of a state or a country. You see yourself as a native of the world, of the whole planet. No matter where you go, people have their prejudices, and look down on others. But people are people, no matter what language they speak or where they live."

"In Vietnam," Johnny wrote to his brother Joe, who also got into the Red Cross, "there are no status symbols to hide behind. You can see a person as he really is. The good are as evident as the greedy or selfish. But my job is to help anyone in need, even if I disagree strongly with his attitude."

In 1970 Johnny was transferred to Frankfurt, Germany.

He and Helge Lehnebach fell in love, and planned their wedding for September 1, 1973. By that time Johnny expected to be in Uncle Sam's consular service. But it did not work out exactly as planned.

Although he did not smoke, Johnny developed a persistent cough. Doctors examined him for TB, but found no trace of it. He went back to work. Then in February, 1973, at an Army hospital in Frankfurt, physicians discovered that the lymph glands in his neck were riddled with cancer.

As soon as Johnny was informed of his condition, although he was not yet thinking of death, he went to the hospital chapel. There he knelt before the tabernacle, and committed himself wholeheartedly to the will of God. He then wrote to his mother and father, "God is outside of time, and I believe He helps us in the right direction. It seems presumptuous to pray for only what we want to happen, as if we know what is best. I think we should thank God for showing us the best way."

His attitude was not tinged with fatalism. He submitted to God's will, and at the same time followed medical advice by taking treatments to slow up the disease and extend his life as far as possible. Helge was aware of the situation, although neither of them anticipated the closeness of death, and still wanted to marry Johnny. They advanced the date, and were married at his parents' home in Colorado on July 14, 1973, by Mrs. Downs's brother, Father Shawn Sheehan.

Back in Germany, a doctor at the Cancer Research Hospital in Heidelberg took a great interest in Johnny, giving him out-patient treatment, and hope. When Downs came for his regular chemotherapy one Wednesday, however, his lungs were congested on account of flu. The doctor said, "I think you had better stay here in Heidelberg for a few days." Johnny agreed, and phoned Helge in Frankfurt.

On Friday he walked into the hospital expecting to get another in a series of treatments. But he never stood on his feet again. Suddenly the light in his eyes began to fade. A German priest was hurriedly summoned. After he received Viaticum, Johnny, who was conscious but confused, said, "Thank you, Uncle Shawn."

Saturday morning, about 4 A.M., on the feast of the Holy Rosary, he died. Inasmuch as Jack and Eileen Downs and their children had been saying the Rosary every day of their family life, the day seemed appropriate.

When his parents arrived in Germany for the funeral, someone they had never met before said, "When I heard about Johnny, I went to Confession for the first time in years."

The first warning came to Lois Krautkremer in June, 1955, a few nights after she finished her sophomore year in the Papillion, Nebraska, High School. She was working at two jobs, selling candy at the local movie theater, and filling cones at the Dairy Queen. She could not have been happier, because every customer was a friend. In her spare time she played softball, volleyball, and tennis. She had always been a tomboy, and seldom sick. She had just started dating, and looked forward to skating parties and pep rallies, dances, and banquets in her junior year.

Then, in the middle of the night, her parents heard her scream with pain. They rushed to her room, and could only learn that her back hurt. The doctor diagnosed a slipped disc. But a few days later both of Lois's legs were paralyzed, and specialists were consulted. Because paralysis had reached the muscles used in breathing, a spinal tap was ordered. The diagnosis: polio. They got her into an iron lung just in time. Her life was in jeopardy.

Next day Lois received the Last Sacraments, and immediately afterward went into delirium. After four days, she regained consciousness, but remained in the iron lung for several months until a chest respirator could be found for her.

"I remember the first day I was out of the iron lung," she says, "using a small respirator. I heard myself trying to say, 'I can breathe.' The therapist was looking down at me with moist eyes. The next milestone was the rocking bed. Finally, by day I was allowed to sit up in a wheelchair with a bantam respirator on my chest. At night I slept in the rocking bed. I didn't realize that polio is more than just a physical problem. It can be a traumatic experience."

During nine months at Children's Hospital and three months at St. Joseph's in Omaha, Lois was isolated. There was no patients of her own age in the wheelchairs. Visitors who got in to see her often became afraid of picking up a bug. Her loneliness was deep.

"When I got home, Mom's nursing and cooking, which had always been superior, were better than ever. But when you are completely dependent, you feel burdensome and useless. It took me a long time to see this as something every polio patient has to live through. I was wallowing in self-pity, and nothing could be more destructive. But after four months at Warm Springs, Georgia, in the winter of 1958–59, I began to get the best of myself.''

She finished high school by correspondence. While taking college courses in the same way, she got a job timing commercials for Radio WOW. She sold Christmas cards by phone, using a mouth stick to dial the numbers. She also used the stick to turn pages, and to type.

''My biggest break came about ten years ago,'' she says. ''A handicapped friend who had been running a hobby shop gave me some oil paints. I had never dreamed of painting a picture even in my healthiest days. But I tried to, just for fun, and painting soon became my first love. It has brought so many good things into my life, like a few awards, and many friends I would never have met otherwise. Recently a TV station did a five-minute feature on my painting. God always opens new doors.''

Since 1970 Lois has been an active member of the Cornhusker Handicapped Club, and has devoted lots of time to St. Columbkille's Parish, Papillion, where she is on the adult education board. She also belongs to a Bible discussion group, and a prayer group. Her favorite quotation is from Isaiah: ''You shall be called by a new name, pronounced by the mouth of the Lord. No more shall men call you forsaken.''

Lois wraps it up this way: ''First, God gave me the healing grace of the Last Sacraments. Then He rescued me from self-pity and sustained me with so many blessings. My one prayer is to remain faithful to this God-given vocation.''

A stray bullet changed Father George Walter King's life.

Secretary to Bishop Thomas Lillis in Kansas City, Missouri, Father King, thirty-eight, was showing a couple of visitors around an amusement park. They all stopped at the shooting gallery, and had a great time shooting down metal ducks. Then somebody dropped a rifle on the counter, thinking it was empty. But it went off. The .22 bullet ricocheted and lodged in Father King's lower spine.

Doctors at St. Joseph's Hospital studied X-rays and concluded the bullet could not be removed without causing death. For the longest year of his life, Father King lay helpless and flat on his back. He then heard the medical verdict, ''You will never walk again.''

Because there was no feeling in his legs, he was taken to Bellevue

Hospital, New York City, for extensive testing. There a second team of doctors confirmed the decision not to touch the bullet. They fitted his right leg with a steel brace, tried him out on parallel bars, and then on crutches. Slowly, painfully, he learned to move himself about. For the rest of his life he suffered abdominal and intestinal problems. Both legs jerked painfully and uncontrollably. He never slept more than three hours at night. But he walked.

When a one-man parish in Higginsville, Missouri, was opened, he asked for the job. His bishop was doubtful, but Father King proved he could offer Mass hanging on to the altar, could stand up for the announcements and sermon on Sunday, and could drive a standard-shift car using his left foot on the accelerator and brake. He got the parish, and stayed there eight years. Then he became pastor of St. Aloysius in Kansas City, and finally of the cathedral, which he completely renovated.

In Kansas City, he represented the diocese in the downtown business and labor community. He knew the city, not only from the Church's viewpoint, but from civic, economic, and social angles as well. Bishop Edwin O'Hara made him vicar general and treasurer of the diocese, and monsignor. Pope Pius XII made him a papal chamberlain.

When he died in 1969 at the age of 68, the Kansas City *Times* noted: "Father King moved through the secular world with assurance and understanding. The spirit of ecumenism was nothing new to him. He saw his disability as a source of strength. His tolerance and good counsel made him one of the most beloved churchmen in the community."

His handicap did not dampen his jovial manner. Several times a week he got to luncheons and dinners where he repeatedly served as master of ceremonies.

President Harry Truman, Mayor H. Roy Bartle, and a host of others were close personal friends and admirers of the monsignor. But he did not allow the great and the wealthy to monopolize all his time.

"George's love for the needy was his hallmark," says Monsignor John J. Murphy, who lived at cathedral rectory with his friend for many years. "Wherever he was stationed his St. Vincent de Paul Society was always active. Whenever he went to visit a poor family, he stopped at a grocery store on the way. He formed a group of businessmen called 'The Arimatheans,' after the man who buried Our Lord, to provide funds and act as pallbearers for the burial of the indigent. And for many years, he himself sent regular financial support to a Christian-Arab family in Jerusalem."

The monsignor had some favorite mottoes. "If life hands you a lemon, make lemonade." "Play the game of life honestly with the cards that are dealt to you." He told Father Rodney Crewse, "Always in my night prayers I say an extra *Ave* that God will give me the grace never to let down a friend."

Some years before his death he formed a charitable trust to continue various works he had sponsored.

At his own request he was buried in a rough wooden box, which was covered with black cloth. His friend and superior, Bishop Charles Helmsing, said, "Even if he had enjoyed perfect health and mobility, he could not have done more for God and men."

When the Good
Die Young

*The tragedy of Joe and Colleen rocked their rural
community*

By ROBERT REILLY

Deputy Robert M. Jordan of the Dodge County, Nebraska, Sheriff's
Office finished typing his accident report:

Killed, Joseph J. Horvatich, 19, Elkhorn; injured, carried from scene,
Colleen Leonard, 13, Elkhorn.

Also injured, but less seriously, was the driver, Dennis L. Anderson, 20,
of Gretna.

1977 Pontiac Grand Prix, brown, totaled. Accident occurred 6:35 P.M.,
Highway 8, east of Fremont, on Saturday, November 5, 1977.

Jordan penciled in the little boxes. *Seat belts?* Yes. *Road types?*
Two-lane blacktop. Surface wet. Dark. Misting. *Driver's apparent con-
dition?* Had been drinking.
Describe What Happened.

Driver stated: "I guess we came to a pretty sharp corner and I must have
missed the corner. I don't know how fast I was going. I think I hit the brakes."

On Friday, Joe Horvatich, Dan Leonard, Dennis Anderson, and two
friends had started for Spalding, Nebraska, in a car and a truck to
inaugurate the pheasant season. Colleen Leonard accompanied them as
far as her grandparents' home. She carried a present for her grandfater,
whose birthday was close to her own. Her brother Dan said he'd see
her Sunday afternoon. But the hunting was bad, and they returned
Saturday afternoon to pick up Colleen.

"My suitcase is in the living room," Colleen told Dan, as if instructing a bellboy.

"You go get it!" Dan chided, pretending to take after her. They both laughed.

She was some kid sister. Always laughing. They were very close.

Colleen rode in Dan's truck as far as Fremont, where everyone took a break. Then, for some reason, she switched to Dennis's more comfortable new Pontiac. They crossed the viaduct and turned east.

Twenty miles to Elkhorn. A dangerous stretch of road, characterized by curves and drainage ditches. Dan, now following Anderson's Pontiac, was concerned. Dennis didn't know this road well. Besides, it was foggy and slick. Dan picked up his CB mike to warn of the bend ahead. Why don't their brake lights go on? He watched the car plunge into the ditch and smash against the embarkment.

"The lights never did go on," Dan remembered later.

John and Aggie Horvatich were sitting down to dinner at the Elkhorn Lanes where they bowled weekly. At 7:45 P.M. one of the employes handed John a note. *Call this number.* Unfamiliar, but it appeared urgent. John and Aggie went together to the wall phone, and Aggie dialed the seven digits.

"I'm sorry. You have not reached a working number. . . ."

Three times she got the recording, then called the operator.

"I can't do anything you're not doing," she was scolded.

The next time a young voice answered. A friend of Joe's.

"Where are you at?" Aggie asked.

He told her he was at the hospital in Fremont. "There's been an accident. Missed a curve."

She inquired about everyone. Dennis? He's okay. They're working on Colleen Leonard. Somewhere. He didn't know where they had taken everyone. Finally—Joe. Joe?

"Joe isn't with us anymore, Mrs. Horvatich."

That simple. Not with us. Anymore. Aggie handed the phone to John, and he collected the details. They left for the hospital.

Pat and Jack Leonard were in Missouri the night of Nebraska's football victory over the Tigers. Two other couples, also "Big Red" fans, were with them, and, as was their custom on this trek, they had driven to Moberly, Missouri, forty miles north, to stay overnight. That's where

Nebraska state patrolman Ken Harper reached them after the state police traced their van to the Ramada Inn. Better that a friend talk to them.

The three couples were just examining their menus when they heard the page calling Jack. Bud Lisko, sensing some problem, went to the phone with Jack. His instincts were right. Bad news.

"Got to go," Jack announced as he hung up. "That was Ken Harper. There's been an accident."

He told Pat and the others what he knew. While they were packing, Jack phoned the Dodge County Memorial Hospital in Fremont. Joe Horvatich, dead, they heard him say. Colleen? Serious. Very serious. They helped each other with the suitcases and, in fifteen minutes, were headed north, then west, to the interstate. The friends handled the driving.

"It was a long ride," Pat Leonard remembers.

Her friends tried to comfort her. Everything is going to be okay. Let's wait and see what happened. Could be a mistake.

About 9:30 P.M. they pulled off the highway. Jack phoned Harper again and learned there had been no response from Colleen. The doctors wanted permission to move her to Methodist Hospital in Omaha for brain scans. Jack assented.

He signaled his friend Bud Lisko into the men's room.

"It's really bad. She won't make it." Bud couldn't say anything. "Let's keep this to ourselves," Jack suggested, as they settled again into the red van.

"But I knew," Pat declares. "I knew something bad had happened."

Earlier that evening, in the rectory of Saint Patrick's Parish, Fremont, Father Rick Arkfeld was watching television. In a few days he'd celebrate his first anniversary here, helping out on weekends. For the two years before that, the forty-four-year-old priest hadn't been stationed anywhere. The official archdiocesan directory listed him as on "leave of absence."

One day in 1974, after a succession of rural parishes, he decided to pack it all in.

"I'm a guy who has to keep busy. I don't really hunt or fish or play golf. I need something to do. At my last place I restored the whole house. Took me three months. But no one ever came to visit."

He traded his car for a pickup wagon, bought a cabin on a sandpit lake near Fremont, then delivered his resignation to his archbishop. His income now came from a furniture-repair business he'd built with borrowed money and a rented facility.

His neighbors at the lake were the Leonards, who drove up every weekend. Often Colleen would bound over to Father Rick's place, shouting: "Hi, Father! Guess what we're having for supper."

The phone rang in the rectory, and a nurse requested him by name. In a few minutes he was headed across town, speculating on who the injured person might be. As he mentally scanned a list of friends and parishioners, he never included the Leonards. But when he reached the hospital room, he spotted Dan.

"Who is it, Dan?"

"Colleen."

Not her, dear God, not Colleen. He anointed her, then questioned the physician. Little hope. No hope, really. Father Arkfeld looked at the neighbors who had gathered. She'll come out of it, they were telling each other. She'll be okay.

There was nothing to do but wait. Right now it was only the machine that was keeping Colleen alive.

During that week, Father Martin J. Petrasic spent a lot of time with the Horvatiches. He knew the Leonards well, too. All were members of St. Patrick's parish in Elkhorn. When Father Petrasic arrived twenty-one years ago, the Leonards and Horvatiches were already there, and the Horvatiches had grandparents who used to walk to Mass on Sunday from their farm.

"Joe was a serious-minded boy," says this youthful-looking pastor. "Like his father, Joe helped out here. An usher, and before that an altar boy, even when he was a strapping young man."

That week he sat with John and Aggie for hours, praying.

He recalls Colleen, too, her visits to the rectory when her father, a plumber, was doing volunteer work for the parish. "One time she was helping him clean up, and I asked her why she was cleaning up when the workmen would only get it dirty again. She fixed me with those big blue eyes and insisted, 'Then we'll just clean it up again.' "

He settles back in the brown leather chair and sighs.

"The fact that it was double is what hits you. One you can take. But not two." He shakes his head.

* * *

Monday should have been a happy day for the Leonards. It was Colleen's fourteenth birthday. Now they were standing over her bed, watching her thin figure bloat grotesquely. She hadn't taken a breath.

On Sunday they had completed three brain scans. And two more today. All were flat.

"We'll try one more," offered the attending physician.

"Doc," said Jack, "if there's no response, why keep her on that thing? There's nothing there."

The doctor looked down at the floor.

"You're right," he agreed. "There's nothing there."

They turned off the machine.

Joe's wake was on Tuesday evening, with the funeral scheduled for the following morning. Then a freak snowstorm blew up, and they had to postpone the funeral until Thursday. Joe would be buried in the morning, Colleen in the afternoon.

The night of the Rosary for Colleen, the roads were coated with glare ice. Some friends and relatives were turned back by the weather, and still the wake was packed.

As Father Petrasic was reciting the sorrowful mysteries, he glanced into the coffin. And wept. He saw Colleen again as the little girl sweeping his rectory. In a strained voice, he continued.

In the rear, in shadow, stood Dennis Anderson. A big, good-natured kid, not knowing what to do. The Rosary concluded.

Father Arkfeld took him by the hand. "Would you like me to go up to the coffin with you?"

"I sure would, Father," responded Dennis.

They walked to the front together, and Dennis knelt down. He prayed a long time. Then he turned, awkwardly, to face the Leonard family. They were all standing, thanking the mourners who shuffled by. Out of the corner of her eye, Pat saw the bewildered youngster. She broke from the line and embraced him.

"We love you, Dennis."

Thursday was bitter cold, and death was on everyone's mind. In the morning perhaps 300 people jammed into St. Patrick's Church, opposite the rectory. Father Petrasic was in the pulpit trying to comfort John and Aggie and the others.

He traced Joe's life as a Christian, spoke of hope and love and the unity shared by them all. He asked them if they imagined for a moment that Christ had abandoned them in their time of sorrow.

"The dear Lord Jesus never forgets his own," he said in conclusion.

Aggie was comforted by his words and by the presence on the altar of monks from Mount Michael. "I don't know what it was exactly," she says, "but something helped. I found a great strength."

That same afternoon, Father Arkfeld began to tremble. He sat listening to the readings, and it dawned on him again that he must preach in a few moments. He had prepared nothing. He tried, but he couldn't get it down on paper. The words of the liturgy passed through his mind.

From Ecclesiastes: "For everything there is a season, and a time for every matter under heaven; a time to be born, and a time to die; a time to plant, and a time to reap . . . a time to weep, and a time to laugh. . . ."

And the Gospel according to John which says that "unless a grain of wheat falls into the earth and dies, it remains alone; but if it dies, it bears much fruit. . . ."

Father Arkfeld tried to pull himself together. He remembered his mother's funeral.

"She had a great send-off. A terrific little Irish lady laid out in a white shawl I bought her years before. The Communion hymn was *When Irish Eyes Are Smiling.* Everybody left that church happy."

He thought of his mother, and when he stood up, he was feeling good. "But I don't know where the sermon came from," he admits. "It's hard to explain."

He heard himself speaking of the spring of the year when the wise farmer plans his work. If you don't think it out, you don't get a good crop. You need just the right seed for just the right soil.

"God is a farmer," he explained. "And he had very rich soil. Pat and Jack. And he had just the right seed. And he planted it in the womb of that good woman. And because he is the best farmer ever, he saw to the harvest. And Jack and Pat helped in all stages of cultivation. They fed her, clothed her, even punished her. They taught her to love and serve God. And they gave her a right to live forever.

"Everything happens in its own time, but we don't know when that time is. So we must sit and wait and be ready. To us, Colleen's death seems untimely, but not to God.

"You all knew Colleen. Then close your minds a moment. Can you hear her laugh? If you thought her laugh was pretty, if you thought her laugh was contagious, can you imagine what she is doing right now?''

It was still enough in that church to imagine such distant laughter. Father Arkfeld waited. He wasn't sure how he would finish. He began by asking them what Colleen would say to this audience if she were there at that instant. Suddenly he found himself speaking, not in the third person, but in the first person. Not about Colleen, but *as* Colleen.

"I loved you," he said. "Mom and Dad, I really loved you. I'm going to miss helping you, Mom, and taking care of you when your back hurts. And, Dad, I won't be able to fetch you a drink any more or bring the footstool for you. But Dad and Mom, don't ask me to come back. My life with you was great, but it was only the beginning.''

John Horvatich stayed home for two weeks after the funeral. It was hard on him. He and Joe had fished together, hunted, talked, argued, watched hundreds of ball games. After those two weeks, he was okay. He even talks again about owning his own farm.

Aggie has done pretty well. "You go along real good," she says, "then something comes into your mind. You think of things he did and see him doing them. Perhaps you cry a bit. And sometimes you can't cry when you want to cry.''

Father Arkfeld sold his business and is building a new house, not far from the Leonards. Friends think he's close to returning to his vocation full time. "What I learned from the Leonards," he states, "was acceptance of the will of God.''

The weekend after the funeral, Nebraska played a home game. And the Leonards looked at their season ticket.

"You go on," offered Pat. "I'll just stay here.''

"Mama," Jack shot back, "we always do things together.''

She looked at him for a few seconds, then nodded. "Life goes on, I suppose, so we may as well get started.''

And they went to the game.

On March 17th, St. Patrick's Church, Elkhorn, held its annual dance. Both the Leonards and Horvatiches showed up.

"I thought that was a great display of faith," says Father Petrasic. "They were announcing a return to life. Remember, these were people who really loved their children.''

There are scars, of course. Dan Leonard still feels guilty because he wasn't with his sister. And Dennis Anderson will take a while to shake his personal sorrow.

Still, in their own ways, Joe and Colleen live on. Joe as a family legend and an inspiration to friends; Colleen as a living part of others' lives.

Before Colleen left Methodist Hospital, a kidney unit arrived, and the Leonards were asked to donate the little girl's kidneys. Pat agreed.

"Now, I understand one of those kidneys is keeping alive a mother with three children. And Colleen's eyes are helping two people to see who were blind from birth. I like to think she is still helping, as she always did."

The Christmas
After Alice Died

Never had I felt more alone, or been more mistaken

By HAROLD MELOWSKI

Util last year, the greatest sorrow of my life was that my wife, Alice, and I could not have any children. To make up for this in a small way, we always invited all the children on our street to our house each Christmas morning for breakfast.

We would decorate the house with snowflakes and angels in the windows, a nativity scene, and a Christmas tree in the living room, and other ornaments that we hoped would appeal to the children. When our young guests arrived—there were usually ten or fifteen of them—we said grace and served them such delicacies as orange juice garnished with a candy cane (which could be used as a straw once it began to dissolve). After the meal we gave each of the youngsters a wrapped toy or game. We used to look forward to these breakfasts with the joyful impatience of children.

But last year, about six weeks before Christmas, Alice died. I could not concentrate at work. I could not force myself to cook anything but the simplest dishes. Sometimes I would sit for hours without moving, and then suddenly find myself crying for no apparent reason.

I decided not to invite the children over for the traditional Christmas breakfast. But I did not have to be alone for the holidays. Kathy and Peter Zack, my next-door neighbors, asked me to join them and their three children for dinner on Christmas Eve. As soon as I arrived and had my coat off, Kathy asked me, "Do you have any milk at your house?"

"Yes," I replied. "If you need some, I'll get it right away."

234

"Oh, that's all right. Come in and sit down. The kids have been waiting for you. Just give Peter your keys and he can get it in a few minutes."

So I sat down, prepared for a nice chat with eight-year-old Beth and six-year-old Jimmy. (Their little sister was upstairs sleeping.) But my words wouldn't come. What if Beth and Jimmy should ask me about my Christmas breakfast? How could I explain to them? Would they think I was just selfish or self-pitying? I began to think they would. Worse, I began to think they would be right.

But neither of them mentioned the breakfast. At first I felt relieved, but then I started to wonder if they remembered it or cared about it. As they prattled on about their toys, their friends, and Christmas, I thought they would be reminded of our breakfast tradition, and yet they said nothing. This was strange, I thought, but the more we talked, the more I became convinced that they remembered the breakfast but didn't want to embarrass Grandpa Melowski (as they called me) by bringing it up.

I didn't have long to ponder this. Dinner was soon ready and afterward we all went to late Mass. After Mass, the Zacks let me out of their car in front of my house. I thanked them and wished them all Merry Christmas as I walked toward my front door. Only then did I notice that Peter had left a light on when he borrowed the milk—and that someone had decorated my windows with snowflakes and angels!

When I opened the door, I saw that the whole house had been tranformed with a Christmas tree, a nativity scene, candles, and all the other decorations of the season. On the dining room table was Alice's green Christmas tablecloth and her pine-cone centerpiece. What a kind gesture! At that moment, I wished that I could still put on the breakfast, but I had made no preparations.

The next morning at about eight, a five-year-old with a package of sweet rolls rang my bell. Before I could ask him what was going on, he was joined by two of his friends, one with a pound of bacon, the other with a pitcher of orange juice. Within fifteen minutes, my house was alive with all the children on our street, and I had all the food I needed for the usual festive breakfast. I was tremendously pleased, although in the back of my mind I still feared that I would disappoint my guests. I knew my spur-of-the-moment party was missing one important ingredient.

At about nine-thirty, though, I had another surprise. Kathy Zack came to my back door.

"How's the breakfast?" she asked.

"I'm having the time of my life," I answered.

"I brought something for you," she said, setting a shopping bag on the counter.

"More food?"

"No," she said. "Take a look."

Inside the bag were individually wrapped packages, each bearing the name of one of the children in the dining room and signed, "Merry Christmas from Grandpa Melowski."

My happiness was complete. It was more than just knowing that the children would receive their customary gifts and wouldn't be disappointed; it was the feeling that everyone cared.

I like to think it's significant that I received a gift of love on the same day that the world received a sign of God's love two thousand years ago in Bethlehem. I never found out who to thank for my Christmas present. I said my "Thank You" in my prayers that night—and that spoke of my gratitude more than anything I could ever say to my neighbors.

The Lady Who Postponed
Her Suicide

. . . and found out why she was alive

By THOMAS H. COSGROVE, C.SS.R.

Eve's dalliance with suicide began early. As a high-school freshman she swallowed a batch of aspirin, trusting it would be as lethal as hemlock. She achieved only nausea.

Two years later, the morbid obsession resurged. Eve found a bottle marked "Poison!" and emblazoned with skull and crossbones. She drank it all and managed to hold it down long enough to sicken herself, but she vomited before the chemical could take fatal hold. She lay ill for several days, and her parents diagnosed intestinal flu.

Incidentally, her mother and father were not unloving or cruel. But feeding a family of ten during the money-meager 1930's distracted them. They failed to perceive that several of their children needed unique attention. And Eve told them of neither her uncanny craze nor her actual endeavors to do away with herself.

Late in her seventeenth year, Eve stopped brooding upon dying and surrendered to the exhilaration of living. Previously, even when her hunger for life had soared the highest, she had sensed the melancholy presence keeping remote watch, ready to move in and reclaim her mind. But, at last, she felt free.

She was surrounded by young men, for, aside from being uncommonly good-looking, she had a coquetry tempered by an intriguing reserve. She enrolled in nursing school, and discovered that nursing was a skill for which she had an easy instinct. Her earliest ambition had been to nourish life and prolong it. Even when she least wanted to live, and even as she actually poured poison for herself, she still blessed the beauty of being. She felt that she alone was unworthy to be.

In her third year of training, Randy arrived in her life, coming romantically from the sea. He was handsome, open, untroubled, energetic, and just beginning a career in the U.S. Navy. Eve saw him as an antidote to her disposition to despair.

Before her marriage Eve's favorite brother called her to say goodbye. Always able to make Eve laugh, he mimicked someone they had known in childhood, and, while she was giggling, merrily announced that he would die that day. They had often spoken of their mutual attraction to suicide, but he seemed, on this last occasion, so full of mirth that Eve did not take him seriously. But after hanging up the phone, he went to the basement and shot himself. He was twenty-two.

Eve was thrown into vivid remembrance of her own thrust toward self-destruction. She had already told Randy of her adolescent actions against her own life; now she suggested she might be carrying an unhealthy strain. But Randy's cavalier confidence soon did away with all of Eve's doubts. They were married in a joyous ceremony. A priest presided, for Randy was stoutly Catholic, and Eve the vaguest kind of Protestant.

When I first met them, a few years later, I was drawn to them. Eve told me her marriage had honed her awareness both of the human and the divine. Her religious education had been hazy, and she was pleased with the precision of Catholicism. With no urging from Randy she was converted and was delighted to learn that suicide is an immoral act. She cherished this teaching as a spiritual weapon against the return of her eerie enemy.

A minor flaw in their marriage was the fierce intensity of their disagreements. But their reconciliations were fervent and immediate. Whether their love was growing up or winding down, I, as a spectator, could never decide.

The major want was their lack of children. They pursued the matter medically, and learned that Randy was so lightly fertile that conception was unlikely. Accordingly, they adopted two boys, an infant and a child of three, keen-minded but with a bodily defect that had made him undesirable to other adoptive parents. Eve gave up work in the obstetrical ward for her own nursery, and wrote to me, "To watch Randy with the kids brings good tears to my eyes."

Randy's joy in fatherhood waned as the boys grew and demanded more of him. Sea duty he had dreaded since his marriage, but now he began to look forward to it. Rising in rank more quickly than his peers, he grew amibitious to progress at a faster pace. Even when shorebound, he volunteered for extra duty. His home grew less attractive when the son of imperfect physique developed alarming behavior symptoms. Psychiatric help was imperative, and this irritated Randy the more. He blamed the boy rather than himself or Eve.

Eve, of course, blamed herself. Twice during these years of decline, she relapsed into her old malaise. She took pills, knowing now exactly how to deal out her own death. After each of these instances, Randy inexplicably appeared, discerned what had been done, and saved her life. Oddly this weakness of Eve's never angered him, and he chided her only with compassion.

Eventually Eve noticed that her husband was avoiding intimacy not only with his sons but with her as well. She surmised that there was another woman. She was right.

Randy chose New Year's Eve, and the last dance of the old year, to tell Eve he wanted a divorce. So when the Navy Club crowd was breaking into *Auld Lang Syne*, Eve was fleeing the dance floor.

Randy was not a theatrical man, nor a sadistic one. He selected the scene, I think, because he feared facing Eve in a thoughtful encounter. She always had the power to make him rethink wild decisions. But, at this turn in his life when he was thirty-eight and could pass for twenty-five, he was recklessly bent on freedom, and would not risk an hour of reflection.

One day I received a call from Eve. She was being driven by the old, sinister impulse. I talked—frantically, calmly, wisely, foolishly. Something I said succeeded in obtaining a stay of execution.

Within five years of the divorce Eve was quite alone. The disturbed son was sent, after counseling failed, to a costly mental center for the young. The younger boy was promising until his adolescence. Then he succumbed to drugs and petty thievery. Ordinary guidance failed to reach him, and Eve, hoping to bring him to normal, surrendered him to an institution.

It was not easy to console her. She told me that, in being separated from her husband and sundered from her sons, she had begun to suspect that God Himself wanted nothing to do with her. But when she promised to delay doing violence to herself, I knew the seemingly remote God was near, for my words alone were too weak to deter her.

Eve fell back on the one thing left to her, and found work as a night nurse in a medical ward. Her expertise as a nurse had always been obvious. But, gradually, it became clear that some power, other than superb tact and technique, was passing from her to her patients.

Dying patients spontaneously began to reveal their reluctance to die, and their fear of the nothingness, or the eternity, that opens beyond final breath and last heartbeat. And Eve discovered that her response relieved, consoled, and actually exorcised them of fear.

Eve did not become evangelistic about her ability and never sought to schedule or repeat her counsel. She waited unanxiously until the dying person asked the question. Then she told what she knew and felt—old truths, to be sure, but seasoned by the long, raw experience of confronting her own death.

Every time this good thing happened, Eve felt herself breaking free, ever so little, of her own fascination with suicide. Her liberation is not yet complete, but continues to unfold. She and I are not distressed at the slow pace of her release, for a disease of such depth and endurance relaxes its grip only gradually.

The most incredible detail of this authentic history is Eve's ability to diminish the fear of death in those who are about to die. Recently she was interviewed by a graduate student researching the human reaction to the dying process. The woman was so impressed, she asked Eve to appear in a university classroom and personally describe the incidents.

The wise and the prudent may say that Eve could have avoided tragedy by seeking professional help at the first symptom of suicidal tendencies. And, surely, this is what she and I would advise anybody who is thinking seriously of suicide.

But I have written this for the man and woman who feel, at times, that they have found more of failure than of success, and who suspect that even their small triumphs may be disguised defeats. It is for those who feel they have no talent to distinguish them from others. While they may never have seriously considered killing themselves, they may have secretly asked the question, "Why was I ever born?"

All of these, and they are not a few, can take heart from hearing of Eve's luckless journey. For flowing from her failure, rising out of her weakness, is an ability of great worth to all men and women.

Acknowledgments

The editor wishes to thank those who granted permission to use in this book the articles listed below.

Efforts have been made to obtain permission for the others, but the copyright holders could not be located. If they are heard from after the publication of *The Catholic Digest Book of Courage*, they will be duly credited in any reprint of the book.

Vernon Pizer, for "Chaplains Who Gave Their Lives"; *The New York Times Magazine*, for "Report from Ladder 17"; Doubleday & Co., for "When the Tornado Took Our House" and "When I Went Looking for Room for Christ"; *Home Life*, for "A Family That Passed Our Way"; The *St. Louis Review*, for "Samaritan to the Sewer Rats"; the estate of Irwin Ross, for "The Doll That Spoke" and "When Leroy Came to Our House"; *Family and Marriage*, for "How Tina Learned She Was Loved"; NC News Service, for "Jenny, Yvonne, and the Secret of Happiness"; Carol Weber, for "Diary of a Reluctant Mother"; *St. Anthony Messenger*, for "I Was Fifteen, Pregnant, and Scared"; *Queen* magazine, for "They've Kidnaped Melissa!"; the *Advocate*, for "The Fischers: Nine Children and Four Races"; E. P. Dutton, for "All God's Children"; Mary E. McKenna, for "I Married a Blind Man"; Marian Hodgkinson, for "This Spring, and Maybe Another"; the *Denver Post*, for "The Doctors Give Me 20 Years—or 20 Days"; the *Lakeshore Visitor*, for "Father Daly's Cancer"; Dale Francis, for "My Last Years with Barbara"; *Friar* magazine, for "John, Lois, and Father George Carry Their Crosses"; *Liguorian* magazine, for "The Lady Who Postponed Her Suicide."

Cowden 11/95